GENEALOGY THEOLOGY

Exploring Family Lines and Spiritual Legacies

Frank G. Honeycutt

WILLIAM B. EERDMANS PUBLISHING COMPANY
GRAND RAPIDS, MICHIGAN

Wm. B. Eerdmans Publishing Co.
2006 44th Street SE, Grand Rapids, MI 49508
www.eerdmans.com

Published 2026
Printed in the United States of America

32 31 30 29 28 27 26   1 2 3 4 5 6 7

ISBN 978-0-8028-8528-9

Library of Congress Cataloging-in-Publication Data

A catalog record for this book is available from the Library of Congress.

Unless otherwise noted, Scripture quotations are taken from the New Revised Standard Version.

"The genealogies, like the purity regulations of Leviticus, are parts of the Bible readers are free to skip, right? No longer. In this highly original and profound book, Frank Honeycutt reveals how the biblical genealogies are must-read material, how they are bursting with human experience and holy wisdom, how they resound like tuning forks through the stories of our lives. Those who read this fine book will never skip over a genealogy again!"

—THOMAS G. LONG, professor emeritus of preaching,
Candler School of Theology

"From its startling opening paragraphs to its stunning final two chapters, *Genealogy Theology* is an arresting read. Frank Honeycutt is besotted with stories—from his own family history, from novels, from the Bible—and he relays them with gorgeous style and grace. Somehow, amid all the dazzling narration, we learn a lot about knotty theological quandaries such as predestination and human freedom. And we will never see a family tree or faded photograph of an almost-forgotten relative the same way again."

—RODNEY CLAPP, author of *Living Out of Control: Political and Personal Faith in Waning Christendom*

"In my years of reading Frank Honeycutt's work, I've learned to sit back and trust the journey. Multiple questions and concepts to mull over will be introduced and just as I'm trying to identify the throughline, Honeycutt skillfully slips in a point that illuminates everything and makes a lasting impression. He is a master at this written sleight of hand. His work in *Genealogy Theology* is no different. Through sharing scripture and his own deeply personal stories of legacy, Honeycutt invites readers on a journey of question, wonder, and compassion as we consider our own inheritances—both blood and divine. The result is a thoughtful exploration of the beautiful mysteries of life and the faith that shapes it."

—MEGAN BRANDSRUD,
former content editor of *Living Lutheran*

"In *Genealogy Theology*, Frank Honeycutt offers a deeply engaging exploration of how spiritual legacies—both redemptive and painful—echo across generations. With his characteristic honesty, warmth, and wisdom, he weaves together biblical insight, personal narrative, and pastoral experience to invite readers into a thoughtful reflection on their own family histories. Eloquent, heartfelt, and thoughtful, this book reveals the quiet power of God and the quiet power of everyday lives."

—MARK POWELL, professor of English,
Appalachian State University

"I did not expect to ever see a book about 'genealogy theology' but I am glad I found this one. Honeycutt has a way of writing as if he were in the room with us, as if he empathizes with all our questions about life. He brings gentle humor to bear on deep questions and does so in a way that puts readers at ease. He shows a modesty toward his subject that rings true; he does not take himself too seriously but does take his theology seriously. I greatly enjoyed this adventure."

—EDWARD DAVIS, professor of geography,
Emory & Henry University

"By using his own stories—his own surprising genealogy—Frank Honeycutt helps us recognize how God continues to work in and through each of us by our baptism into Jesus's genealogy, to make a way where life that really is life (1 Tim. 6:19) becomes possible and real. A must read for pastors and congregations as well as those who seek, or are skeptical of, what God is up to these days!"

—PAUL PINGEL, pastor of Grace Lutheran Church (ELCA),
Waynesboro, Virginia

For Cindy, as we celebrate 45 years of marriage . . .

. . . who believed in this book long before I did

CONTENTS

Introduction

THE WONDER OF THE SEARCH

"O LORD, you have searched me and known me."

—*Psalm 139:1*

In December of 1908, a temporary wooden gallows was hammered together within a short walk from the town square of Concord, North Carolina, about thirty miles from Charlotte. The bleak apparatus of execution—constructed for a black man named Will, convicted before a jury of raping a sixteen-year-old white girl, Pearl—attracted close to two thousand people in curious and gawking assembly, a week before Christmas, for the last (legal) public hanging in state history.

The young sheriff, elected a month before, was only thirty-six. Like 90 percent of the Cabarrus County population at the turn of the century, the lawman was Lutheran, several members of his extended family fairly recent immigrants from Germany. Progressive agriculture techniques brought from their homeland were extremely successful over the decades, creating envy and imitation. The sheriff attended worship every Sunday in nearby Gold Hill and afterward, around a large table of extended kin, enjoyed the good food grown and gathered from well-tended land.

There was talk among family members that the sheriff was torn over the execution, before and after, harboring private suspicion that the accused man was innocent. And further talk that he opposed capital punishment in any form, influenced by the pastor who taught him Luther's *Small Catechism* in Gold Hill as a teenager.

The sheriff protected the infamous inmate until the day of the hanging, shuttling Will to safety in Raleigh after a lynch mob threatened to burn down the Concord town jail. And then he arranged for his safe return to the county where a badge conveyed authority and respect among so many Lutherans. The sheriff's wife, Agnes, volunteered to sew the condemned man's gallows hood, an act of mercy and charity, many thought.

The crowd gathered that morning, holiday wreaths on several doors of nearby businesses. Will was executed at 11:16 a.m. Justice prevailed in the eyes and hearts of the assembly, who returned home feeling safer, I suspect. The sheriff walked home for a late lunch, two blocks away, relieved it was all over.

The sheriff's name, incidentally, was J. Franklin Honeycutt, my great-grandfather, Frank, for whom I am named.

*

There is a small creek near our house in Walhalla, located in the northwest corner of South Carolina not far from the Chattooga River, straddling the Georgia–South Carolina state line, a national scenic waterway made famous by the James Dickey novel and subsequent film *Deliverance*. A local friend knows the guy who plays the grinning porch-picker, part of the famous banjo duet that opens the movie.

The creek near our house deepens with the latest hard rain but becomes quite shallow in the hot days of a southern summer. On regular walks—never missing a Sunday stroll after church in any weather—I stop at a roadside perch above the creek, lean against the guardrail, and look into the water about eight feet below, spilling into a pool from a concrete culvert.

I am searching for fish, fascinated with all things piscine since early childhood, convinced as a five-year-old that with patience, a hook, and a long line, I could toss a baited rig out the window of our family car into a passing body of water and reel in a whopper upon arriving at our destination.

My wife, Cindy, occasionally drives by my solitary creek perch and slows down when she notices her husband peering into the water with a focused, undistracted gaze. Surprising me in automotive stealth, she once rolled down the window and yelled, "There's no fish in that creek, you lovable nut job!"

It took me months of searching to finally see them—waiting for cloudy water to clear, watching at the right time of day for the properly angled sun to eliminate both glare and shadow, illumining depth. I reported the discovery to Cindy, who accused me of lying, which I sometimes do, I'll confess. Nothing important; small fibs, detectable falsehoods, to keep things spicy.

But there they were, after months of patient searching in the same pool, which was also never quite the same with each visit—three small fish, each about two inches long, darting around as if performing in my old teenage aquarium.

I'm convinced there are more, waiting patiently to reveal themselves.

*

This is a book about searching, both divine and human. How God searches for and somehow has in mind the marvelous intricacies of any life through divine genealogical foresight via the multitude of choices that we and our relatives make (and could have made). And how we, in turn, inevitably search back toward God, wondering about our place in a vast cosmos, realizing at some point in our passing years how if a single small facet of the past (with one of a variety of colorful forebears) was changed—just a tiny smidge of time tinkered with and altered—none of us would even be. Where such past decisions have led any of us boggles the mind in creative consequence, shaping the unique individuals we've come to be, still in process.

I decided to enroll at Clemson University, for example, a freshman in the fall of 1975. But had I attended Auburn, which came very close to happening, I'd have never met my wife at a certain Lutheran summer camp a couple of years later, and our three rather unique children would have never entered our young family. I'd have never met a welcoming campus pastor called "Rev," who greatly influenced a subsequent decision to enter seminary—an idea for an adolescent church dropout and budding chemical engineering major that was absolutely absent from even the fringes of his vocational radar screen at age eighteen.

Factor in dozens of similar choices, hundreds, from my ancestors and yours. That I'm writing these words—and you are reading them as an equally unpredictable human being who could describe your own marvelous and seemingly random intersections from the past—is nothing short of head spinning.

The fact that any of us, all of us, *are* is miraculous. Equally ponderous is that we almost *weren't*.

Is it hopelessly naive to believe that God's very eyes "beheld my unformed substance" (Ps. 139:16) and that the days I've been given were somehow known by a loving, divine, and creative Omniscience, ahead of time, "when none of [those days] as yet existed"? What does this reveal about the vast territory of the mind of God?

Does such a claim by the ancient psalmist also suggest some sort of human puppetry at play? That our ancestors unwittingly (or wittingly) succumbed to a series of divinely authored forks in the road, with God perhaps not entirely removing the gift of human freedom in the matter, but indeed teasing out a beautiful ballet of choices resulting in the complicated, gifted, layered, and mysterious reader of this book, a person like you?

These are the sorts of questions we'll tackle together in the chapters to come. Questions concerning inherited illness and inherited incident and how both shape varied inheritors (like us) who follow a long genealogical line much of which has been received as gift (and possible burden), somewhat out of our planning or control. Questions concerning destiny, chance, and free will and how "free" any of us really are to shape our present and future. And questions pointing to the ecclesiastical genealogy of God, birthing new people (a "new creation," 2 Cor. 5:17) in baptism through the church, which theologically reframes what any of us may have inherited.

Two stories, in particular, have nagged at me for decades, giving birth to the idea for this book. One from my father's side of the family concerning my great-grandfather, the public executioner mentioned above, Sheriff Frank of Concord, over a century ago, a man I've never met whose grainy photograph still seems to follow me around our den, suggesting an unsettling lack of concord inside the man, not to mention his great-grandson. I'll share more of this story and the role of inherited incident in anyone's life in chapter 4.

And a second story concerning my great-aunt Eulie, whose nervous breakdown in 1927 after a year of college in Texas became a source of embarrassment for her family, not an uncommon occurrence at the time. Eulie lived in a state mental hospital near Memphis for over fifty years and was lobotomized (perhaps experimentally) during the period. My mother was unaware of her aunt's existence until discovering documents in the North Carolina attic of her childhood home after my grandfather (Eulie's brother) died in 1973, a discovery that unlocked a long generational genetic predisposition for mental health challenges on Mom's side of the family. I'll share more of this story in chapter 3, specifically the role of inherited illness passed on genetically through many generations.

Stories like these still shape our days and lead to ponderous questions about God and how any of us came to be. There is surprising peace experienced in the search, I've found, even when we cannot make sense of it all.

Though scientific discoveries will not be discounted along the way, the pages to come will centrally find shape through my own pastoral vocation, the stories and genealogies of the Bible, and insights guided by the prodding of the Holy Spirit, still interceding on our behalf "with sighs too deep for words" (Rom. 8:26).

Sighs, I'm convinced, are a wordless form of prayer. Like hidden fish rising from dark shadows after months of waiting and watching, these stories often require a patient search with new eyes looking well below the surface of anyone's history.

In Paul Harding's incomparable novel *This Other Eden*, an early twentieth-century interracial island community on the Maine coast survives poverty and intense weather with old stories grounded in love. Esther, the matriarch, has just finished telling the incredible family-defining story of escape from a terrible hurricane, a great flood that rocked the island in September of 1815. It's a very cold winter in Maine; the supply of firewood is running low. The story Esther tells her family warms them and reminds those around the waning fire of the varied couplings that brought them all to the island: "fourth, fifth, and sixth generations' distillate of Angolan fathers and Scottish grandpas, Irish mothers and Congolese grannies, Cape Verdean uncles and Penobscot aunts, cousins from Dingle, Glasgow, and Montserrat, the wind thumping, the snow swirling, their stomachs growling, their toes and fingers burned black to icicles, crowding the cooling woodstove . . . thrilled and hallowed by the story they all knew as well as the one from the Bible. Better, even."[1]

Stories of loving survival shape and color any family inheritance. I've never survived a hurricane, nor have any of my ancestors, to my knowledge. But the stormy stories I'll share in this book will undoubtedly conjure others from your own genealogical past, hopefully assisting your own search for meaning and truth.

Chapter 1

THE GENEALOGY OF JESUS

"Do you work wonders for the dead?
Do the shades rise up to praise you?"

—*Psalm 88:10*

Perhaps due to Jesus's unusual birth, I suspect many Christians do not think much about the importance of genealogy in his life. "For us and our salvation he came down from heaven," asserts the Nicene Creed, "was incarnate of the Virgin Mary and became truly human."[1]

He came down from heaven. One could forgive a new disciple of Christ for assuming that Jesus miraculously appeared in a specific place and time, his earthly parents only drafted into action as attentive and temporary caretakers for their gifted child's early years and adolescence until his public ministry began with an unmistakable voice of baptismal affirmation from heaven, clarifying his true origin (Matt. 3:13–17).

Curiously, however, Matthew's Gospel begins not with the famous Bethlehem birth but instead with a detailed genealogy (1:1–17) filled with a cast of colorful characters covering centuries of time. Just after his baptism (and right before Jesus enters the wilderness to confront temptations from a wily nemesis), Luke's Gospel also trots out the ancient family tree (3:23–38), as if to say, "You're going to need this family pictorial directory, Jesus, before embarking upon such a dangerous mission."

The two genealogical lists are notably different and proceed in different directions according to time, but both serve as reminders that Jesus was not magically inserted into history apart from a band of buried and illustrious relatives whose stories shaped and guided him. Jesus was born into a specific family inheritance chock-full of tales and details that gave birth to his world-changing ministry of inclusion and good news for sinners and outcasts. Part of Jesus's lasting appeal is that he, like any person of faith, inherited a vast array of family events—some carrying outsized consequence, others fairly humdrum—overseen by a God who, according to journalist Judith Shulevitz, "resides in commonplace things; his sublime purposes course through the small-bore tragedies of unremarkable people, to be revealed in the fullness of time."[2] This theological assertion is an important key to unlocking percolated meaning in anyone's colorful genealogy with past purposes (shaping the present) waiting to be revealed like those hidden fish in our neighborhood creek. They're there all along but sometimes slow to be discovered.

"We do not live to ourselves, and we do not die to ourselves," Saint Paul would later claim for a band of fledgling Christians drenched in local history (Rom. 14:7). Both statements (living and dying) also applied to Jesus's ministry that led to a cross. Jesus was not a self-made savior. He did not drop from heaven into human history inherently knowing everything required to fulfill his purpose and destiny. "Although he was a Son," Jesus "learned obedience" (Heb. 5:8). He also learned about life and how to answer God's arduous call from his many forebears in stories told in synagogue, around a family fire, and at bedtime as a child. Jesus was undoubtedly precocious even in puberty, yes, but not preprogrammed. He inherited a bevy of fascinating ancestors and their colorful lives of faith.

When Jesus was twelve, separated for three days from his worried parents during a Passover visit to Jerusalem, his parents "found him in the temple, sitting among the teachers, listening to them and asking them questions" (Luke 2:46). Surely he was asking questions about the stories handed down in his wider Jewish family, and his perception of his place in their future meaning was growing. Jesus's parabolic teaching style, his pastoral ministry of radical inclusion, his penchant of taking risky less-traveled roads, and his courageous consistency in speaking truth to power can all be linked to kin that kindled the content and direction of his days. (These four vocational characteristics will be explored in the next section as we delve into the curious genealogy listed in Matthew's Gospel.)

One of my favorite modern Lenten hymns, "Bless Now, O God, the Journey," was written by a Canadian hymn writer, Sylvia Dunstan, who died of liver cancer at a young age, not much older than Jesus at his death. She served as a prison chaplain and magazine editor during her short career. Here's verse 1 from her hymn:

> Bless now, O God, the journey that all your
> people make,
> The path through noise and silence, the way of
> give and take.
> The trail is found in desert and winds the
> mountain round,
> then leads beside still waters, the road where faith
> is found.[3]

The hymn, reflecting Dunstan's own path of service and early death, draws upon repeated biblical themes and stories featuring a cast of her scriptural forebears. Jesus also drew upon past stories featuring the inner and outer spiritual geography of engagement, silence, waterless times, and revelatory peeks from peaks, all creating a certain way of sacrificial living, the way of the cross, into which he invites modern disciples.

✶

Several English versions of the Bible use the word "genealogy" in the first verse of the New Testament (Matt. 1:1). The family tree of Jesus is then described in three fourteen-generation divisions. Abraham, David, and the deportation to Babylon mark the major dividing points in the genealogy, a word that appears as *genesis* in the original Greek of Matthew's Gospel.

The same Greek word is also used to describe "the birth" of Jesus (Matt. 1:18), probably an intentional hearkening back to the book of Genesis and the Bible's opening pages. A new origin story, a new lens to help make sense of the world, is beginning. An additional implication seems to be that any "birth" is always dependent upon a colorful cast of relatives and their unusual stories.

Five women are mentioned over these generations—Tamar, Rahab, Ruth, "the wife of Uriah,"[4] and Mary, mother of Jesus. That alone is unusual, as women were rarely mentioned in first-century genealogies, surely a foreshadowing of the important role of women in the ministry of Jesus in all four Gospels. Also noteworthy: the first four women were not born into the favored Jewish family line; that detail, too, hearkens forward to the radical baptismal theology of the New Testament where elevation of ethnic purity is replaced with a new ecclesiastical genealogy creating a different family where "there is no longer Jew or Greek" (Gal. 3:28), a familiar but still breathtaking claim.

These easy-to-overlook details are like bits of bread dropped along a winding path, important clues for the biblical sleuth, subtle invitations to look further. Such detective work in the Bible will be good practice for anyone planning a deep dive into their own genealogical past. Be patient, keep searching. Insight often surfaces slowly, both in the Bible and in the long beauty of any life. There are many stories to be mined in Matthew's genealogy of Jesus. Here are four ministry characteristics that Jesus likely inherited from four female kin from his past.

1. *Jesus's Parabolic Teaching Style: An Inheritance from Tamar*

Tamar, the first woman mentioned in Matthew's genealogy, is the mother of twins (Perez and Zerah)[5] born in an unusual, shocking fashion that might garner a modern movie an NC-17 rating. Her story is found in Genesis 38. (Please take a moment to read this chapter in total. Trust me, it's enticingly strange. I've lured several non-Bible-reading friends onto the road toward biblical fluency with this single titillating chapter alone. And again, keep your own weird genealogical history—perhaps waiting to be discovered—in mind as you read.)

Notice that Genesis 38, contextually, seems to be a bolt out of the blue, oddly interrupting the Joseph narrative that seamlessly continues (see 37:36, then 39:1) if the chapter under consideration were omitted entirely. It's as if a stack of scribal index cards containing these old stories got this chapter out of place after they all fell to the floor. King David will hail from this bizarre sexual coupling (as will Jesus), but still—chapter 38 seems like a jarring intrusion in the main Genesis plot.

The chapter is laden with lascivious details. Judah's intermarriage with a foreign Canaanite woman (38:2). The behavior of their firstborn son (Er), who wickedly erred (sorry), inciting divine execution (38:7) for unclear transgressions. The reluctant Onan (number two son), drafted by Judah to "perform the duty of a brother-in-law" (38:8) and impregnate Er's grieving wife, Tamar. Three consecutive strange details. But wait, there's more.

Hesitant Onan's semen is spilled on the ground "whenever" (multiple attempts!) he had halfhearted sex with his brother's wife, later creating the word "onanism." (Look it up, a euphemism for masturbation in many dictionaries.)[6] This sexual spillage displeased the Lord. Onan, bizarrely, is also put to death by the Lord for, presumably, wasting semen and balking at the whole plan (38:10). Can this chapter get any weirder? Yes, it can.

Two of Judah's three sons are dead. A third son, Shelah, is (at least initially) too young for desperate Tamar. Perhaps panicked at the thought of childlessness in a culture that severely judged such, the great-great-great-great (and then some) grandmother of Jesus resorts to an extreme plan of action.

Shedding her widow's garments, Tamar disguises herself as a cultic prostitute, a creative ruse to get pregnant by her father-in-law. On a sheep-shearing trip to Timnah,[7] Judah quickly arranges sex with a woman whom he doesn't recognize—yes, Tamar, his daughter-in-law, undercover. Judah will eventually settle up and pay the "prostitute" with a young kid from his flock, leaving his staff (no pun intended), signet, and cord as escrow. Think what you will of Tamar, but Judah is also utterly complicit in the tale's rather abnormal genealogical outcome.

Three months later, upon discovering that Tamar is "pregnant as a result of whoredom," Judah (who has yet to make the connection) initially hits the roof and self-righteously commands his daughter-in-law to be brought out and burned (38:24). Yikes. Tamar quickly produces the escrow proof, Judah confesses, and twins are born of the union, but not without an amusing and dramatic final twist involving a "crimson thread" (38:30) tied to one infant's wrist. This boy waves his hand into the world, then retreats back into his mother's birth canal, yielding to his brother and creating a bit of birth-order confusion, shades of Jacob and Esau and their struggle inside Rebekah's womb (Gen. 25:19–28).

Got all that? One chapter, thirty verses, loads of intrigue, and then immediately back to Joseph and his travails with Potiphar (and his lying wife) in Genesis 39. I suppose so many strange details—their cumulative weirdness—could have been conveniently omitted by a prudent Genesis editor. And what about Matthew's brief allusion to this convoluted pregnancy in his curtain-raising genealogy of Jesus? That too could have been glossed over or omitted entirely using only the father's name for the twins rather than (again, unusually) adding Tamar's. But this proverbial bit of bread was dropped, clue-like, into Jesus's family tree, almost inviting a careful reader to search further.

Take a well-earned break from the biblical action. A genealogical sleuth like you can now faithfully ask: *What in the world might all this mean for the future ministry of Jesus, who surely heard this provocative story growing up?* Please imagine an impish and precocious child Jesus asking his parents at bedtime: "Can you tell me again the old story of Grandma Tamar and how she became pregnant with those twin boys? Please leave nothing out." Like any set of parents deciding which family stories to share and emphasize at what age, Mary and Joseph perhaps maintain brief eye contact, raise eyebrows with pursed lips, and begin again.

Jesus became a renowned storyteller largely because he grew up with great stories—tales of liberating plagues involving amphibians and insects that eventually freed his people (Exod. 8); a reluctant queen who finally found her confrontational tongue, silenced a court sycophant, and saved her family (Esther 4); a great prophet who rat-tailed a river, parting it, then passed his leadership garment to a young protégé before flying away into heaven on a chariot in a fiery whirlwind (2 Kings 2); a talking donkey who spoke sense into his wayward owner, who was on the verge of a huge mistake (Num. 22); a weepy and reluctant servant of the Lord who buried his underwear beside a river—then dug it up—to symbolize people who didn't cling closely to God (Jer. 13); a witch skilled in necromancy whose scary séance riled the prophet whom she called up from the dead (1 Sam. 28); a young boy who outwitted and killed a haughty giant with a homemade slingshot (1 Sam. 17); and many more stories of heroism, valor, and faith. These stories surely shaped the boy Jesus's theological imagination and childhood precocity well before he showed up in the temple, three days gone from Mom and Dad, with a bagful of good questions for his theological elders. Jesus grew up with nuanced and layered stories full of symbolism and hidden meaning. Old narratives resisting easy interpretation, told daily, that lingered in the imagination of a young boy.

The parables Jesus would later tell found shape and texture in the complex stories he inherited. The word "parable" has an interesting etymology. Derived from *para* (alongside) and *bolē* (a throwing), the word suggests inherent creative friction as disparate ideas are tossed into proximity with one another, creating literary sparks and new ways of looking at the world. The stories Jesus told stayed with his listeners because they were open-ended, inviting ponderous and percolated interpretation long after they were first heard. Like a good sermon, a parable includes theological "homework" to be completed outside the space in which it was shared. A parable is often filled with delayed meaning, intentionally so, partly to stimulate a listener's interpretive skills. Jesus refused to spoon-feed truth to his listeners. He wanted them to dig, which inculcates lasting truth.

It can be argued that a parable's interpretive homework is never finished, forever worked out in the lives of listeners who both embrace and sometimes resist its layered truth. We never discover if the prodigal and his pissed-off, self-righteous brother ever reconcile. We do not learn if the disgruntled grape pickers who worked all day eventually get over the scandalous equal wage paid to those who worked only an hour. We hear nothing more about a legalistic lawyer whose moralistic Scrabble board is upended by a surprising Samaritan hero (an oxymoron to Jesus's first listeners) who radically loves an enemy.

The story of Tamar and her shocking pregnancy ploy resists easy interpretation. I suspect a young boy like Jesus, full of curiosity, was absolutely enthralled with the story's many unusual details. In all their colorful complexity, Tamar and the characters of Genesis 38 are a great genealogical fit for the unusual storytelling style that would mark Jesus's own ministry narrative—outcasts surprisingly included; marginalized people finding an unexpected way where there doesn't seem to be a clear solution or path forward; a double dose of grace in the weirdly born twins, echoing Jesus's own unusual birth that included community whispers, surely overheard by a young child. And, as he aged, born to die, the "red thread" of a Savior's blood coursing through many of the stories he heard.

Such parabolic stories—with seemingly unconnected and unusual details creating their own friction and consternation with delayed meaning—are waiting to be discovered in your own genealogical line. These stories and details may have been suppressed by your protective forebears. In concert with Jesus's odd cast of family characters from the past, the stories are an important part of you, nonetheless.

2. *Jesus's Pastoral Ministry of Radical Inclusion: An Inheritance from Rahab*

The fall of Jericho and its famous crumbling wall is another story that undoubtedly captured Jesus's childhood attention. Our own children requested to hear the unusual narrative elements of this tale many times.

Encouraged by God to cross the Jordan and take possession of divinely promised land, Joshua sends two men to spy on the current occupants. They do quite a bit of undercover reconnaissance work, but their mission seems to pale in importance to the courage of the creative and prescient prostitute who senses the future, confesses God's reign over heaven and earth, and hides the men on her roof (Josh. 2:1–24).

The spies in this story are never named. Rahab's fame will eventually spread to three distinct mentions in the New Testament—her appearance in Jesus's genealogy (Matt. 1:5) as one of his great-great-great (and then some) grandmothers; her impressive commendation as an example of living faith (Heb. 11:31); and her shining example of good works (James 2:25).

Unlike Tamar, whose situational harlotry was limited to a single desperate role as a disguised cultic prostitute (a livelihood intended to appease the local Canaanite fertility gods), Rahab seems to have chosen prostitution as a full-time secular profession. She welcomes the two spies into her home, a residence "within the wall itself" (Josh. 2:15). This strategic location possibly appealed to her customers' need for a quick and clandestine getaway and would also assist in the spies' eventual escape by rope.

The "crimson cord" tied in Rahab's window (Josh. 2:21) to signal future sanctuary grabs my attention as a possible literary connection to the previous story, the "crimson thread" figuring in the birth of Tamar's twins. Both images conjure thoughts of liberation and freedom for these two women, however oddly accomplished. I do not mean to imply that these original Jewish stories in any way foreshadowed the "crimson" freedom of Jesus's ministry. But I do not discount that Jesus, looking back for hints of his own past identity, may have found power in their colorful details, shaping his own blood-red cord of compassion that liberated all of humanity.

Genealogically speaking, to claim a full-time prostitute as one of his central ancestors must have informed how Jesus would welcome people into his orbit of care and inclusion. He surely shocked the theological elite of his day with the accusation that "tax collectors and prostitutes"[8] were more receptive to the gospel and the coming kingdom than his own respected religious elders and mentors (Matt. 21:31).

God's unexpected and circuitous intentions—embraced by Rahab, a single woman[9] who made her livelihood through unconventional means—also will draw the likes of Zacchaeus, a despised and wealthy tax collector (Luke 19); Mary Magdalene, possessed by seven demons (Luke 8:2); an unnamed woman at a well, whispered about by her neighbors (John 4); and a couple of brothers, James and John, known as "Boanerges" (literally, "Sons of Thunder"),[10] not to mention many others with unusual pasts and character.

Walls indeed will tumble down in Jericho with Rahab's wily and unexpected assistance. In Jesus's own ministry—welcoming outsiders, preaching unity and peace—he will "[break] down the dividing wall" separating people, the "hostility" (Eph. 2:14) often foisted upon the outsider.

Did Rahab's unusual story—and her scant mention in Jesus's genealogy—shape the ministry of her great-great-grandson and Matthew's subsequent rendition of the gospel? Another bit of bread dropped along the path. File it away as you make sense of Jesus's origins and continue to ponder your own.

3. Jesus's Penchant of Taking Less-Traveled Roads: An Inheritance from Ruth

The book of Ruth opens during a famine. Displacement and a desperate search for food drive a young family of four to leave their homeland, not unlike many refugees on the move in the early twenty-first-century who are looking for stability, safety, and a new start.

They settle in Moab, east of the Dead Sea, about seventy miles away via a rocky trail through mountains; this is quite a trek from their home of Bethlehem, a word that literally means "House of Bread." Perhaps a lot of now-unemployed bakers lived there due to the famine. I've always loved the eucharistic implications in this village name that would become the birthplace of Jesus centuries later, but this epic story of another great-great- (and then some) grandmother—also surely told and retold to a little boy like Jesus—is initially driven by hunger.

And eventually by premature death. Fleeing poverty, Elimelech, Naomi, and their two sons settle and thrive for about a decade in a foreign land that famine has not touched. Both sons intermarry with young local women of Moab. Say it—the word "Moabitesses" pleasingly rolls off the tongue.

Ten happy years pass. At the end of the decade all three men in the family die (we aren't told how), leaving three vulnerable widows who make important decisions concerning their uncertain and worrisome future.

The book of Ruth also begins with a revelation of biblical context: the action occurs "in the days when the judges ruled" (1:1). Flip back a single page in your Bible to the ominous final verse of Judges: "all the people did what was right in their own eyes" (Judg. 21:25). Certainly a verse worth pausing over when pondering the surprising decision of a young woman who boldly bucked what was "right for her," instead choosing, sacrificially, to leave her homeland and accompany her foreign mother-in-law over the mountains and back to Bethlehem, a week's hilly walk that surely seemed like a journey to Timbuktu.

Naomi is returning to her homeland, an aging foreign widow completely out of options. Orpah and Ruth pledge to accompany her. Twice Naomi stops in mid-trail and tells her daughters-in-law to turn back and go home.

With words as famous as any in the Old Testament, still familiarly used in wedding liturgies and anniversary celebrations, Ruth says,

> "Where you go, I will go;
> where you lodge, I will lodge;
> your people shall be my people,
> and your God my God." (1:16)

Unlike her sister, who understandably did what "was right in her own eyes," Ruth refuses to return to her country of origin. She "clung" to Naomi (1:14), an intimate word of loyalty and trust also used early in the book of Genesis (2:24) to describe the lifelong promises and marital union of a man and a woman.

Ruth's decision, in retrospect, is both admirable and loyal. It's important not to miss that the decision is also shocking and norm busting, surely a genealogical curiosity for Jesus and his family as they told old stories from the past around the fire. As Naomi arrives with Ruth, back in Bethlehem after a decade away, we're told that "the whole town was stirred because of them" (1:19). A long-departed woman and her foreign daughter-in-law—both widows, traveling alone through mountains—set tongues wagging. They were definitely an oddity.

Ruth's genealogical influence can be seen in Jesus's ministry as an adult. I'm thinking of the time that Jesus heads to the coast (presumably for a bit of rest and relaxation) and encounters an intrusive gentile mother with a persistent request. Jesus is on the Mediterranean (take a moment to locate Tyre on a map) as this story unfolds, perhaps for a minivacation, "and [does] not want anyone to know he [is] there" (Mark 7:24). And who can blame the man? He was human, besieged with requests, and needed time away incognito. Perhaps he's sipping a glass of good local wine on the back porch of some seaside cottage, wearing a big hat, when this worried mom discovers the healer is in town and throws herself at the weary man's feet.

Her daughter has a demon. Don't all adolescents have demons? I've known many mothers whose worry for a teenage child might cause them to interrupt the motorcade of a dignitary if there was a chance the famous person could be of assistance. Her insistence is not surprising. She's desperate.

A bit jarring is Jesus's initial refusal to help on the grounds of ethnic boundary: "Let the children be fed first, for it is not fair to take the children's food and throw it to the dogs" (7:27). *She's not one of us. And I'm on vacation.*

The mother persists. Jesus relents. The daughter is healed.

I'm impressed with the mother's persistence. And Jesus lauds her for it. But there seems to be a turning point in Jesus's ministry here on this junket to the coast that may be attributed to an awakening understanding of his own genealogical identity. He continues to cross ethnic boundaries in the very next story, healing a foreign deaf man. And the following chapter opens with a second mass feeding of thousands, this time on the gentile side of the Sea of Galilee (8:1–10). Mark's Gospel, near its conclusion, employs a Roman centurion, yet another boundary-breaking character, to offer a rather stunning confession of Jesus's divinity at the foot of the cross: "Truly this man was God's Son!" (15:39). Jesus's disciples never come close to such a confession; only a foreigner.

How instrumental was Ruth in awakening Jesus to a ministry that became far wider and more inclusive than it was at the onset? The young woman from Moab—clinging to a mother-in-law who was not her nationality, embracing a land and its people that were not her own—may have stirred Jesus to a wider perception of his own calling as he attempted anonymity on that coastal back porch in Tyre. Genealogical tidbits from the past have a way of shaping anyone, including Jesus presumably, in profound and unexpected ways. The elders of Bethlehem, toward the end of the book of Ruth, seem to recognize how odd this tidbit truly is as they offer this blessing for Ruth and her new husband, Boaz, that hearkens back to a previous example of God's strange ways: "may your house be like the house of Perez, whom Tamar bore to Judah" (Ruth 4:12). May *your* weird family be blessed like *that* weird family.

What if Ruth had embraced local conventional wisdom and returned to Moab along with prudent Orpah? Change that single decision among dozens of lifelong decisions. (Enroll me, similarly, at Auburn instead of Clemson long ago.) Would Jesus's own ministry have drifted in a different direction? With Tamar and Rahab, Ruth is mentioned in Jesus's genealogy (Matt. 1:5) for a reason. She's a great-great-grandmother who dared to cross boundaries, shaping her great-great-grandson from Bethlehem, who walked through Galilean hills and changed the world with his radical ministry.

4. *Jesus's Consistency in Speaking Truth to Power: An Inheritance from Bathsheba*

In Jesus's genealogy, Bathsheba is mentioned only as "the wife of Uriah" (Matt. 1:6). Of the four women under consideration, she's the only great (and then some) grandmother of Jesus who is referenced solely through her husband. She is also the only member of this four-woman cast who does not speak. Perhaps the story was so salacious that Matthew chose to reveal its place in Jesus's genealogical line through a sort of cryptic nod, a cloaked bit of dropped bread.

The details of the story are indeed shocking. King sees a beautiful woman. King wants this woman, even though she's married. King impregnates the woman and arranges for her husband (Uriah) to be killed in battle (2 Sam. 11–12). In such a time, Bathsheba undoubtedly had little opportunity to resist David's advances.

A servant of the Lord behaves treacherously. The baby conceived from this illicit union will die (2 Sam. 12:12–14). A future child, Solomon, will be born to David and Bathsheba, establishing a line of kings in the second major division of Jesus's genealogy (Matt. 1:6–11). Jesus was born into a royal line where he would become "King of Kings." This tale, in all its perverse darkness, foreshadows the fallen world into which Jesus was born to save.

Joseph Heller (1923–1999), the witty fiction writer, wrote a marvelous novel about the king's life, narrated by David throughout. Here is David, many years later, looking back upon the sordid event in Heller's novel *God Knows*:

> What was a horny young king like me to do when a radiant treat like Bathsheba laid it all out for me to see that eveningtide from the roof of my royal residence? I did what any normal, virile tyrant would do. I saw her, I sent for her, I lay with her, and as simple as that was the imperceptible drift into the turbulent and depressing second half of my life, with its succession of tragedies for which virtually nothing I had undergone had prepared me. . . . I could say that the Devil made me do it. The Devil always comes in handy that way, doesn't he?[11]

Unlike the three women previously mentioned, Bathsheba's role is largely silent in driving a narrative populated by powerful men. But her place in Jesus's genealogy is still vitally important.

David repents. Psalm 51 (which includes a fairly descriptive introductory reference to the famous tryst) is among the most poignant prayers in the Psalter.

> Create in me a clean heart, O God,
> and put a new and right spirit within me.
> Do not cast me away from your presence,
> and do not take your holy spirit from me.
> Restore to me the joy of your salvation,
> and sustain in me a willing spirit. (Ps. 51:10–12)

Liturgies of various traditions have used these words as a weekly offertory for centuries. Jesus no doubt learned as a young boy, perhaps from this very event, that no sin, no transgression, was beyond forgiveness with accompanying repentance.

But Jesus was also shaped and spiritually formed here, I suspect, by the importance of speaking truth to power. Without Nathan's prophetic confrontation of David using the story of a powerful rich man who took advantage of a vulnerable shepherd in poverty (2 Sam. 12:1–10), the king may have escaped exposure for his wrongdoing and any subsequent repentance that led to change.

Did Jesus have this story in mind as he confronted religious hypocrisy in the Gospels with truth and candor? Did he recall Nathan's chutzpah when speaking up to the likes of Pilate and Herod? Bathsheba may be silent in Jesus's genealogical imagination, but her vulnerability spoke loudly in his many encounters of defending those who had no voice.

*

Four women from Jesus's past, each a genealogical grandmother to the subsequent savior of the world. Surely their stories shaped him, told and retold around home and hearth. Matthew chose to include these four women in a long list of male ancestors of Jesus. For them to be mentioned at all in an ancestral list was unusual for that time period.

These four grandmothers shaped various aspects of Jesus: his teaching style (Tamar), his sense of radical inclusion (Rahab), his penchant of choosing less-traveled roads (Ruth), and his courage before the powerful (Bathsheba). I do not believe that Jesus dropped into this world preprogrammed for greatness, even though his divine connections are clear. He was also fortunate to inherit a cast of colorful forebears, "a cloud of witnesses." "Therefore, since we are surrounded by so great a cloud of witnesses, let us also lay aside every weight and the sin that clings so closely, and let us run with perseverance the race that is set before us, looking to Jesus the pioneer and perfecter of our faith, who for the sake of the joy that was set before him endured the cross, disregarding its shame, and has taken his seat at the right hand of the throne of God" (Heb. 12:1–2).

On a walk in our neighborhood recently, I was struck by the abundance of maple seedpods—those parachute-like whirligigs that spin and glide on the wind, landing randomly—falling in nearby woods and along the road berm. (They're technically known as samaras.) I've loved watching the flight and twirl and landing of these pods since childhood. There may be a tendency for ponderous humans like us to believe our lives occurred and emerged like those maple whirligigs, utterly by chance, given what we know of biology, happenstance, coincidence, or sheer luck. It's easy to fall back on the self-made model of human destiny. Thrive solo where you randomly land.

I've always appreciated the honest table prayer offered by the father in the film *Shenandoah* (1965). It's a hard life—dawn-to-dusk work—in Virginia at the dawn of the Civil War. Charlie Anderson (played by Jimmy Stewart) reluctantly promises his dying wife that he'll try to keep God central in the family's future. Here's Charlie's honest dinner prayer offered one evening at the end of a long day: "Lord, we cleared this land. We plowed it, sowed it, and harvested it. We cooked the harvest. It wouldn't be here, we wouldn't be eatin' it if we hadn't done it all ourselves. We worked dog-bone hard for every crumb and morsel, but we thank you just the same anyway, Lord, for the food we're about to eat. Amen."

The reading above from Hebrews challenges assumptions of a self-made, bootstrap future like that envisioned by Charlie Anderson. The "cloud of witnesses" for any human being who attempts to probe the past may be murky and downright overcast at times, but my theological assumption is that even Jesus did not find his own way, solo, miraculously dropped into human time with certain gifts. He had a family, a colorful lineage, a cast of ancestors whose foibles and exploits offered a variety of reflective character traits for a young man barely thirty years old. His specific genealogy mattered mightily in his ministry. Matthew sends a clear signal to readers in this regard by starting his gospel with a long list of names, specific biographical details. Without these names, Jesus's ministry may have taken an altogether different path. Even his words on the cross—forgiveness for his tormentors (Luke 23:34); a redefinition of "family" suggested to his mother (John 19:26–27); and inclusion of a criminal executed alongside (Luke 23:39–43)—cannot be interpreted apart from his genealogical inheritance. I cannot help but believe that Jesus's genealogy helped him face the cross, "disregarding its shame."

The same passage from Hebrews also suggests that peering into the past at our own cloud of preceding witnesses serves to assist anyone's liberation from "every weight" in this life and "the sin that clings so closely," not to mention the added gift of "perseverance" in our unfolding existence, the "race" toward meaning and fulfillment set before us all (Heb. 12:1).

Jesus's genealogy was indeed unique and different. A case can be made that *anyone's* genealogy is also surprisingly odd and filled with strange (and liberating) incidents waiting to be discovered. The search for meaning down through the decades of inherited details is exceedingly important, vital for health and vocational clarity. A further question, however.

What does such a marvelous chain of time and detail reveal about God—and God's creative personality and thinking—in bringing any of us to life?

Chapter 2

BEHOLDING UNFORMED SUBSTANCES

"Your eyes beheld my unformed substance.
In your book were written
all the days that were formed for me,
when none of them as yet existed."

—*Psalm 139:16*

"There is actually no such thing as atheism.
The only choice we get is what to worship."

—*David Foster Wallace*

It's a rather risky (and perhaps presumptuous) theological endeavor to attempt to probe the mind of God. As if God's mind and how it might work is anywhere close to my own flawed and cumbersome brain circuitry.

> For my thoughts are not your thoughts,
> nor are your ways my ways, says the LORD.
> For as the heavens are higher than the earth,
> so are my ways higher than your ways
> and my thoughts than your thoughts. (Isa. 55:8–9)

A pretty clear testimony—be amazed, the conventional prophetic wisdom seems to suggest here. Observe wonder; give thanks for your next breath. But probing what makes God tick? It's prudent to leave such whimsy pretty much silenced alongside Isaiah's wise prophetic claim and move on.

There are several instances in the Bible, however, where God changes the divine mind as a result of human interaction and intercession. Before the ancient twin cities of Sodom and Gomorrah are wiped out via divine wrath, Abraham intercedes in a darkly amusing series of exchanges, talking God down six straight times (if I'm counting correctly), contingent upon the bold old man identifying only a handful of righteous folk in the entire region (Gen. 18:22–33). After the golden calf incident, the Lord's ire again raised, Moses reminds God of the divine job description and again talks God out of what he has in mind. "And the LORD changed his mind about the disaster that he planned to bring on his people" (Exod. 32:14). Jesus suggests that nagging the dickens out of a righteous judge (God) may affect justice, resulting in a changed divine mind through sheer and brassy persistence (Luke 18:1–8).

I suspect these biblical instances reveal why many people have prayed for centuries for certain outcomes: to change God's mind, to shape the course of an uncertain future, and to bring peace instead of anxiety. That God's mind is situationally malleable due to human interaction and consistent plea is well documented in the Bible.

Less clear (and certainly mind-boggling) are other claims concerning the mind of God, like the one that opens this chapter. I'm assuming that the psalmist is not just observing that his own singular "unformed substance" (and nobody else's) was known by God for quite some time before the psalmist was born. This psalm suggests divine knowledge of any of us well before a doctor or midwife ushered the roughly eight billion inhabitants of the planet toward our first breaths, not counting all those who returned to dust before us through natural causes or various calamities. Say what you will about artificial intelligence and its staggering potential to catalogue, mimic, document, file, and predict. If the psalmist's claim is accurate, the mind of God and the divine capability of beholding my own unformed substance—not to even mention the unformed substances of my global companions and antecedents—are enough to dwarf AI in scope, data collection, and sheer jaw-dropping awe and wonder.

Of course, it's possible to believe the psalmist is quite full of it and reject such a theological premise from the get-go. Even faithful pastors of my acquaintance (heck, even me at times) sometimes draw the line at such broad all-knowing claims, wondering if such divine knowledge borders on arranged puppetry with God shaping and pulling all the various strings that brought any of us to this day and these breaths.

I've always loved a Miller Williams poem about a young preacher who stands over an open grave. He knows what the mourners have come to hear, but he's not quite sure what to say. The pastor in that cemetery is absolutely certain of only two things: "my present discomfort" and "how to spell my name." The preacher finally asks himself what any honest Christian must also confess: "How are we so sure of so little after so long?"[1]

Is it possible to believe in the promises of Psalm 139:16 without resorting to arranged divine control over our lives in which we have absolutely no say? "Stepford humans" with zero freedom to resist?

In a wonderful hypothetical exchange, theologian Matthew Myer Boulton imagines a chat with his deceased father, Wayne, who thought a lot about the controversial topics of providence[2] and predestination in the last years of his life. Matthew discovers that "what's caught me off guard most about death is how porous it can seem. . . . Going through Dad's papers was like having a conversation with him."

> FATHER: Human freedom is the freedom to create our own destiny. But at the same time, on another level, that very destiny—the same one we freely create—is also freely given to us by God as a gift, and by definition, a gift is prepared in advance. . . .

SON: But doesn't that end up being a form of puppetry? God lays out the path in advance, and then we're the marionettes, with no choice but to follow the path?

FATHER: No—the puppetry analogy fails because it assumes two distinct, finite entities, the puppet and the puppeteer, operating on the same level in a way that's mutually exclusive. . . . As the Creator of time and space, God isn't bound by temporal and spatial constraints. As the Spirit of life and freedom, God indwells human beings, acting in, with, and through us in ways that enliven and empower us, not that dominate and cancel us out.[3]

Probing the mind of God from a genealogical perspective is daunting.

How weighty to me are your thoughts, O God!
How vast is the sum of them! (Ps. 139:17)

Now there's an understatement. But I find Boulton's imagined father-son exchange compelling, and it inspires five additional observations from the psalm that may shape our reflections concerning the mind of God in relation to any genealogical inheritance.

1. *God knows my thoughts* (Ps. 139:2). I once had a very bright confirmation student named Derrick, about thirteen at the time. It was a small class that year—one guy, two girls. We were having a discussion about the inner life, prayer, and other spiritual disciplines that form us as disciples. How dark thoughts can often shape actions, and how God not only notes our actions in this life but also whether God has access to our random and sometimes unhealthy thoughts. We looked at a few Bible texts, including Psalm 139:2, suggesting that God did indeed have such access. Derrick's eyes opened wide with raised eyebrows. He looked at the girls and then glanced nervously at his pastor and my coteacher,

Mark. His reaction was amusingly transparent and honest: "I'm not so sure I *want* God to know my thoughts!"

I can certainly sympathize with Derrick. But if Jesus is correct in reversing the conventional wisdom of his day—that holiness, sanctification, occurs from the inside out rather than as an attempt to avoid a list of taboos and no-no's (see Mark 7:14–23)—then perhaps it's wise to allow and even invite God to have access to my inner thoughts and imagination, an often dark arena from which I usually shield even my spouse and close friends. It's also important to acknowledge that if God has had my "unformed substance" in mind all these centuries, why not invite a divine embrace of my entire personality, the hidden and even unhealthy parts, to allow Christ's spirit to shape me more and more into his likeness? Such access, over time, links us to the communion of saints in light and better attunes us to their struggles and successes in attempting to follow Jesus during their own time on this earth.

2. *God searches out my path ahead, aware of my peculiar ways and habits* (Ps. 139:3). This doesn't mean that God controls the route ahead or pulls certain divine levers that compromise the gift of human freedom. I think it means that God is constantly searching out healthy possibilities for any of us, attempting to "reroute" his baptized beloved (using GPS lingo) after certain decisions turn out to be boneheaded and unhealthy.

I really did almost go to Auburn to study chemical engineering instead of Clemson. And had I made that choice, my present life would be markedly different. Not necessarily miserable or sad, just very different. You, I suspect, could make a similar declaration with similar past decisions. It's fascinating to imagine *exactly how* life would be changed upon tinkering with one or two past choices.

Piggybacking on the previous point (divine access to my inner life), I'm convinced in retrospect that God knew the best place for me as a result of knowing me so well, providing the divine nudge to head to the upstate of South Carolina instead of eastern Alabama. It's not that I had no choice in the matter. I am willing to say that God knew ahead of time that this would be the best choice given the divine "acquaintance with all my [odd] ways." And those are often a basketful of turbulence and colorful psychopathologies. (More on that later in chapter 3.)

3. *God knows what I'm about to say* (Ps. 139:4). This divine claim affirms respect for human freedom (even more than the other four in this list). To have divine foreknowledge of the many verbal gaffes, insults, angry invective, and malicious gossip that find regular articulation on my forked and often-acidic tongue and *still* allow the gaseous consonants to make their way into unsuspecting nearby eardrums is nothing short of miraculous forbearance and heavenly patience.

4. *God sees through even my favorite hiding places* (Ps. 139:7–12). In 1942, Margaret Wise Brown published the enduring children's classic *The Runaway Bunny*. Our three kids asked for the book over and again, well after they'd "outgrown" it. Beautifully illustrated by Clement Hurd, the book depicts how a young bunny finds a series of hiding places via intent, mischief, or consequence. The loving mother bunny searches and finds her child every time, suggesting there is *nowhere* the little one could go to escape powerful maternal love. Brown has suggested that she had Psalm 139 in mind as she wrote the book, especially verses 7 through 12. "Where can I go from your spirit?" asks the psalmist. "Or where can I flee from your presence?" (139:7).

The divine search described in this psalm surely includes the flights of attempted hiding in a geographical sense, but also flights into myriad psychological facades any of us erect to escape the truth about ourselves. I suppose such unveiled transparency may cause part of us to invoke (with Isaiah) the ancient prayer of one who's just been exposed and caught: "Woe is me! I am lost" (Isa. 6:5)—lost in my inadequacy, my sinfulness, my less-than-stellar past. Isaiah soon discovers that God has searched him out so aggressively not to smite the poor guy for all his flaws but instead to give him a new call, a new direction.

I've always loved the story of Peter and his pals who embark on a night-fishing expedition after Easter (John 21:1–14). They are not supposed to be fishing, please recall, at this point in their vocational lives. Jesus has given his disciples clear marching orders to now fish for people. An odd detail of this story in a gospel laden with symbolism and double entendre is that Peter is found fishing in the nude (21:7) by Jesus as he calls to his disciples from the beach. Maybe Peter was simply hot that night and needed to air out his privates. But I think John wants us to reflect upon the possibility that Peter has figuratively been caught by Jesus with his pants down, caught in his rather rebellious decision to return to his old job.

When Peter finally recognizes who it is on the beach calling his name, I suspect the poor guy probably offered some equivalent of Isaiah's forlorn and woebegone prayer of penitent exposure before the divine gaze. But please note what's waiting for Peter, who pulls his pants on, oddly, before diving in and swimming toward the beach—not a stern lecture, no reprimand for abandoning his clearly stated call, and no reference to his rebellion at all.[4] What's waiting on Peter is breakfast with Chef Jesus (doubling as an expert angler), who offers words and actions that powerfully echo those experienced for centuries by Christians at the Eucharist: "Jesus came and took the bread and gave it to them, and did the same with the fish" (John 21:13).

5. *God intricately weaves my hidden and unique genetic inheritance* (Ps. 139:13–15). Regardless of how one feels about the many issues these verses raise concerning reproduction and fertilization practices and related decisions of anguish concerning unwanted pregnancies, not to mention the many compelling voices on all sides of national abortion debates, these verses make powerful claims concerning the divine power of God, who knows us right down to our unique DNA, right down to "my inward parts" (139:13), organs both hidden from view and often prone, genetically, to relative inherited health or (perhaps) inherited illness. All this marvelous

genetic mystery (known and unknown) may be hidden to human view but not to God's divine gaze.

> My frame was not hidden from you,
> when I was being made in secret,
> intricately woven in the depths of the earth.
> (139:15)

Pause over this verse, please, which reveals divine initiative that eclipses human knowledge in a fantastic subterranean setting and conjures (even symbolically) a more spectacular creative backdrop than any best-selling fantasy novel.

Psalm 139 reveals these five remarkable claims concerning the active mind of God, shaping related issues of providence and genealogical ponderings in anyone's life—God has access to our inner lives, searches out the path ahead, knows the content of our conversations, exposes our hiding places, and creates our respective hidden innards. Our creeds reveal not only a God who created a remarkable world in all its wondrous variety but also a God who creates its complex inhabitants and refuses to leave them alone with their private thoughts and actions. It's all quite a bit to take in and digest—not only the job description and mind of God but also God's relentless presence in our lives, "goodness and mercy" following[5] (even pursuing) me "all the days of my life" (Ps. 23:6).

Is this good news or bad news for a thoughtful genealogical sleuth? Depends, I suspect, on one's perspective. Take Jeremiah, for instance, the reluctant prophet, who resembles the psalmist under consideration in several ways:

> "Before I formed you in the womb I knew you,
> and before you were born I consecrated you;
> I appointed you a prophet to the nations." (Jer. 1:5)

It would be interesting to interview Jeremiah, dozens of centuries removed from my present life (creeping toward seventy) but still remarkably with us as a genealogical witness for many who are called to speak for God. Here's an attempt to examine how Jeremiah might have felt about his predestined and seemingly arranged call to be a prophet.[6]

*

When the yellow buses roll each fall, I remember my elementary schoolteachers and say a prayer of thanksgiving, recalling each name and face. Mildred Chaffin, my fifth-grade teacher at Elbert S. Long School in Chattanooga, was a major player in shaping my early perceptions of God. You did not fool around in Mrs. Chaffin's class. You did not laugh or ever horse around, and even on the playground only guardedly so. It took only a direct gaze from her to address any hint of disorder or rebellion—a gaze I was certain could crack granite. We sat in robotic rows and hardly ever moved from fear of her, sharpening pencils and moving through the lunch line in timed precision like a small platoon of marines. I would rather have wet my pants than ask to go to the bathroom at an unscheduled time. Woe to the poor child who accidentally passed gas during geography.

I came to associate Mrs. Chaffin with God, who could somehow see and know everything even when facing the blackboard. This was 1967, and she preached in class occasionally, using the Bible to undergird her convictions. Once Mrs. Chaffin asked me to serve as class monitor, which was supposed to be something of an honor, but your friends hated you for it. You sat up front at the teacher's desk and took names. "I'll be down the hall for just a minute," said God, "and I know you'll be very good boys and girls, especially since Frank is in charge"—the little snitch.

I still wonder about a boy named Kenny. I wonder if he's in prison. Kenny phoned in a false bomb threat when we were in junior high. All the boys (how gender-biased was that?) were paraded into the gym. Policemen wanted a confession from somebody. They led Kenny away.

During my half-hour tenure as hired informant for God, Kenny ran to the blackboard and with manic glee repeatedly spelled a variety of four-letter words, even the shocking ones, erasing them with each daring gallop. It's hard for a class monitor to ignore this.

God returned to class soon enough. She knew something was up. All eyes rested upon me, and then on Kenny, who was rather large for a fifth grader, and back again to me. I still sometimes wake up in the middle of the night, sweating from this memory.

The thing about serving as a prophet (a pastor like me is sometimes called to this role) is that you are forever stuck between what God wants and what the people want. It's a rather tiring vocation. I'm not sure anybody ever really volunteers for the job. Consider Jeremiah, called to be a prophet while he was still in his mother's womb.

Well that sounds special, like something you might find on a Hallmark card, but here's my take on God's gestational action with Jeremiah. Perhaps he called the old boy to be a prophet when he did because a baby cannot object. "Go, young Jeremiah, and say things to wayward adults that will get them hopping mad." You've got to hand it to God. A small child who cannot even talk will have a hard time questioning this commission.

Jeremiah did not have an easy life in trying to be faithful to God. I suppose that's true for any of us, but Jeremiah had a particularly tough time of it because God said something like, "Okay, class, I'm going to be down the hall and away from you for just a little while. I've appointed Jeremiah to serve as class monitor, and he'll be my ears and eyes and mouth."

Many people ran back and forth to the blackboard, so to speak, during the prophet's tenure, and he had to take names. People got mad, threw him in stocks (Jer. 20:1–2), tossed him into a cistern with three feet of mud in the bottom (38:1–6), called him names and smacked him around. Jeremiah was even instructed by the Lord to remove his underwear, bury it near a rock by a river, then dig it up as a symbol of the unfaithfulness of the people—they weren't clinging closely enough to God as good underwear should (13:1–11). Thank God that Mrs. Chaffin did not ask me to do this.

It was no kind of life, this prophet's life. So even though Jeremiah could not talk back to God in the womb, in chapter 15 we find that the old boy has had enough of the prophetic life. Jeremiah gives it to God with both barrels. He asks God to smite his opponents. He blames God for his sufferings. He recalls the past delight in the relationship, which is no longer delightful. He complains about his isolation, citing his complete lack of a social life. (I can't imagine the prophet ever attending anything resembling a wild party, but Jeremiah reminds God he's never once had fun because of this ridiculous calling.) At prayer's end, he bluntly describes God as a dry creek bed.

> Why is my pain unceasing,
> my wound incurable,
> refusing to be healed?
> Truly, you are to me like a deceitful brook,
> like waters that fail. (15:18)

There is no amen at the end of this prayer, which suggests that Jeremiah has more to say but won't say it.

Years ago my wife and I were hiking the Appalachian Trail in Pennsylvania. It was a very hot and dry summer. We were each down to a single swallow of water. The guidebook assured us that a spring was just ahead on a side trail. I took our water bottles and climbed down a very steep trail, one-quarter mile, to the spring. It was dry—bone dry.

"You, God, are like that useless spring," prayed Jeremiah. "Dry, untrustworthy."

This is quite a prayer. I'm pretty sure that if somebody burst into our quiet, controlled liturgies and prayed this prayer with prophetic vehemence and unbridled despair and volume, we might ask an usher to call the police. But God listens to the one whom he has called from the womb. God allows Jeremiah to vent about the vexing parts of Jeremiah's job. God surely knows exactly how hard it is to be a prophet.

But God also speaks, and Jeremiah receives a direct answer from God concerning his complaints. You might expect a bit of patience and understanding from God—maybe a moment of handholding or six weeks of therapy on someone's couch for the tired prophet. But there is none of this.

"Look, mister," God seems to say. "If you turn back from this nonsense you're mouthing, I'll take you back. I know these people. They're going to fight against you, but they won't prevail over you, for I am with you to save and deliver you" (15:19-20, paraphrased).

God needs the prophet. The prophet is downhearted, but God needs the prophet to speak. The prophet is worn out, but God needs the prophet to speak to ungrateful people. The prophet needs a reminder.

Garret Keizer gets to the heart of Jeremiah's weariness: "The thing that makes us the most angry with God, more angry than droughts and famines, male pattern baldness and cellulite, is God's mercy."[7]

It is the mercy of God—the love of God for his people—that has driven the prophetic vocation in any century. We need prophets. We need people who tell us what we don't want to hear. God sends them back in there. Pray for the Jeremiahs, for those who stand between God and his people.

I am no prophet. I'm often a weary pastor who knows that Kenny still lurks in the pew, waiting to accost me at the church door or in a board meeting. Perhaps Jeremiah's old and honest prayer will temper my vocational timidity and give me the courage to name what needs naming around the school that is church.

*

Jeremiah's witness, alongside the author of Psalm 139, reminds me that even though God knows each of us intimately (recall those five divine attributes above, gleaned from the psalm), we are not forbidden or prevented from rebellion and prayerful sassiness in our respective journeys in this world. I'm not ruling out divine chastisement and correction in response, but in no way are we prearranged automatons unable to resist God's intentions for us if that's our temporary (or permanent) intent.

I used to occasionally use a large chunk of Psalm 139 at funerals, but would always omit the last verses, ending the reading at verse 18. Here the tenor of the psalm abruptly shifts and the narrator pretty much loses it with prayerful vehemence toward enemies and those who are driving him crazy.

> O that you would kill the wicked, O God,
> and that the bloodthirsty would depart from me.
> (139:19)

A startling change in tone, especially given what's come just before. The psalm continues in a similar vein for several verses and then concludes with the author's personal self-examination.

I'm still not sure I'd use these concluding verses in a funeral—not enough time to unpack and explain—but I do have newfound respect for their inclusion in the psaltery despite their abrupt caffeine-like change in tone. Similar to Jeremiah, the psalmist is allowed to rant. The psalmist is allowed a green light to go off-script even given the marvelous and intimate relationship just described in the previous eighteen verses. And again like Jeremiah, God is invited back into the important process of self-examination. God remains the agent of leadership and guidance "in the way everlasting" (139:24).

I'm writing these words at the end of the Easter season, four days before the Day of Pentecost, a remarkable narrative with paranormal and vivid details, but chiefly memorable for me because Peter, of all people, is the guy who stands in the streets of Jerusalem and speaks up, finding his once timid tongue (Acts 2:14–21). Fifty days before, the accusations of two servant-girls around a kindled fire send the same guy into the shadows of fear and lies (Matt. 26:69–75). As predicted, a cock crows, and the full denial is complete. Peter flees into the darkness of his deception, weeping bitterly.

Fast-forward fifty days. Same guy, same streets, same dangers, but now Peter is preaching a sermon of all things within a stone's throw of that fire and those accusations. Here he lives up to Jesus's prediction as "the rock" upon which the church will be built (Matt. 16:18). But, Lord have mercy. To predict the very foundation of the church upon the shaky witness of people like Peter (and the psalmist and Jeremiah) is a profound testimony that God uses unreliable and developing voices like these (like mine) in a fashion that is certainly guided by divine intent but never controlled or preprogrammed.

✶

A couple of key verses in Paul's letter to the Ephesians have always taken my breath away concerning the range of God's work in our lives: "Now to him who by the power at work within us is able to accomplish abundantly *far more than all we can ask or imagine*, to him be glory in the church and in Christ Jesus *to all generations*, forever and ever. Amen" (Eph. 3:20–21). I've highlighted several words here because they so beautifully illustrate the suppositions I'm making in this chapter and indeed throughout this book.

The work of God in our lives exceeds anything we can ask or imagine. Where we've come from (and where we are going) will run into human limitations of partial insight and veiled understanding. Perhaps this is something of a gift. Knowing the entire story might be simply overwhelming in its many details, twists, and turns.

At the same time, any genealogical search is a creative invitation to employ both verbs penned in that letter to the church in

Ephesus—asking and imagining, a promise for the church "to all generations."

The two chapters that follow will ask God to help me make sense of events I did not experience and two people I've never met, both, however, a large part of my chemical and ethical makeup in shaping the pastor I've become. These divine requests—I'll call them two lengthy prayers—will require a bit of holy imagination, several reconstructed facts leading to a few best-guess conclusions concerning a great-aunt with severe mental health challenges and a great-grandfather who was an actor in meting out unsettling "justice" as a young sheriff. From these two individuals hailing from different sides of my immediate family, I hope to make several conclusions that might guide the theological twists and turns in any peek into the past, including yours.

Chapter 3

GENEALOGY AND INHERITED ILLNESS

"They say that these are not the best of times, But they're the only times I've ever known."

—Billy Joel, "Summer, Highland Falls"

"This is my Father's world, and to my list'ning ears all nature sings, and round me rings the music of the spheres."

—Pastor Maltbie Babcock (1858–1901), who committed suicide at age forty-two

My mother's father was a brilliant and funny man. A graduate of Georgia Tech in electrical engineering after World War I, he carried scars from the war—gas-mask combat encounters in the Black Forest of Germany—that he sometimes psychologically masked with a fondness for gin and retreats upstairs into an impressive library of books. He was witty and smart, loved tinkering, and possessed a particular admiration for Benjamin Franklin, whose complete works I inherited from Granddaddy. It took me years to decode his trips with my father to "the post office" as visits to the local VFW to hoist a few cold ones and tell stories with his local pals, many of whom had lived through horrific pasts of their own.

Visits to my grandparents in western North Carolina were rather idyllic and included trips into Pisgah Forest to the fish hatchery, breakfast cooked in the woods over an open fire, and hikes along the Blue Ridge Parkway near Mount Pisgah (elevation 5,721 feet), named for the peak mentioned in Deuteronomy from which Moses glimpses the promised land (Deut. 34:1–4) after forty years of arduous leadership to get there. Moses is only given a peek from this tall peak due to what I've always considered punishment for a minor infraction concerning a rather innocuous order from the Almighty.

Such veiled glimpses into the distance are appropriate metaphors for any family, including mine, attempting to make sense of the passing decades.

Soon after his death in 1973, my mother discovered a secret that her father had been hiding from his three daughters for over fifty years. He had a sister, Eulie, who suffered a severe mental breakdown as a young woman and was subsequently admitted to a state hospital in Tennessee near Memphis, where she spent most of the remainder of her life. Eulie was not mentioned in family conversations—ever. Mom never knew she existed until stumbling upon documents and photographs in an old attic file cabinet in the days following my grandfather's death.

Such secrecy (and shame) concerning mental illness was rather common at the time. As a nation, we are still dealing with the effects of such secrecy, thankfully exposed by scientific discoveries leading to pharmacological assistance coupled with genealogical research that has helped us understand the long entwined genetic inheritance of such illness from various forebears who suffered many of the same symptoms.

Replacing the supposed inadequacies of a lone individual—often creating family shame for (and embarrassment about) that loved one—such discoveries have slowly brought light to centuries of darkness. I have heard it said that we've learned more about mental illness and its incumbent personal wounds in the last twenty-five years than in the last five hundred.

My mother was able to slowly piece together a few facts about her aunt, details bequeathed to her three sons in a spiral-bound book (about many generations of ancestors on both sides of the family) titled *A Search for Yesterday*, a great gift to each of us. She gained access to Eulie's records and was even able to schedule a visit not long before her near-comatose aunt died.

The short story that follows is a constructed interplay between time periods throughout Eulie's known and secret life. Several details (settings, names, dates, and incidents) are factual, but the story itself is largely fictional, shaped in ways that I imagine it may have happened given what my mother discovered. It was important for me to write the story, especially for reasons that will become clear later in the chapter where I'll attempt to make theological observations concerning inherited illness in my own family and perhaps yours.

AUNT EULIE

East of Memphis, 1927

A car pulls to a stop in the shadow of a four-story building that blocks the light of the setting sun on a chilly afternoon in late autumn. The driver looks for a moment through the windshield—up toward the roof, where he notices someone standing at a room window on the third floor—and turns slowly into a graveled parking space.

Two male attendants emerge from the heavy front door, walk down a short flight of steps, and stand ten feet from the trunk of the car, looking straight ahead, neither smiling nor frowning, placed dutifully and ready to assist the driver and his wife with their daughter's luggage.

This is where they'll say good-bye.

Sam steps out of the driver's side and wants to stretch but doesn't. He looks at his shoes and then nods, wordlessly, to the two men. He quietly closes the car door with a soft click that could almost be mistaken for the care a father might take in tucking his child in for the night with a warm quilt.

He walks a few paces from the car, looks up again at the darkening building, lights coming on in several of the rooms. Sam recalls the brochure prepared by the state department of mental health: "Staggered wings on each floor extending outward from the center, resembling the wingspan of a bat." He did not find the description helpful, but it looked about right.

Florence hesitates in the car, still in the front seat. She closes her eyes, offers a silent prayer that seemed longer to Sam than it really was, then touches her eyes with a small handkerchief. She turns and looks into the backseat.

The young woman is looking out her window at the trees, a grove of tall, arranged oaks. She notices that the sun illumines only the tips of the uppermost branches. They seem almost on fire in contrast with the lower limbs. She does not speak to her mother. And she will not offer words to anyone the rest of the day. Their eyes do not meet even when Florence promises that she will never stop loving her youngest child and will visit whenever they are permitted. The mother reaches toward the backseat for her daughter's hand. The reach is not returned.

The two men stand at the daughter's car window for several moments. The shorter of the two opens the door, lowers his head, and nods a smiling greeting. Sam opens the trunk and removes a single suitcase.

The mother and father are both standing outside the car now, holding hands, then embracing. Tears splotch the dry gravel in the silence of the falling darkness.

Each attendant lightly holds one of her arms. The men hesitate at the top of the stairs in front of the big door, whispering something to the young woman who has not resisted their assistance since departing the backseat.

She enters the building and does not look back.

Genealogy and Inherited Illness

Brevard, NC, Summer 1974

She climbs the creaky stairs to the attic, alone in the house where she grew up. The same stairs she once quickly descended for dates with old boyfriends, for hikes in Pisgah Forest, and for hot chocolate around the Christmas tree in the room with so many books. The same stairs she could once navigate blindfolded before leaving for Chapel Hill, sometimes hopping over the last three all at once on her descent.

On the fifth stair, she pauses at an airy opening in the wall—a glassless window used to help ferry soup to the upstairs sick—and looks into the dining room. She makes a face like those she once made at her two younger sisters, imagining her family gathered around a very old wooden table. Ruth stands there for several moments, recalling where each sister sat, her parents at opposite ends, Mother closest to the kitchen. She sticks out her tongue, for fun, and continues her climb, allowing the memories to flood back.

Her Ohio sister, Kate, will arrive soon. They'll begin the slow sifting of stored photographs and papers, filed relics she'd never explored, a chore she'd been putting off since her dad's death last August.

Ruth tries several keys and enters the walk-in attic. It's hot and stuffy, compliments of a warm spell in the North Carolina mountains. She waves through several cobwebs, pretends to dance with the undressed mannequin her mom once used in their dress shop. Crossing the warped floorboards, avoiding a raised nail, she raises the far window then pulls the metal chain hanging from a bare light fixture, unsurprised the bulb is bad.

Late afternoon sun angles into a corner of the attic near the file cabinet. She finds a chair and starts with the bottom drawer. Time passes, two hours—lots of photos, old receipts, birth and marriage certificates, hundreds of letters, and a name she does not recognize, recurring many times.

CHAPTER 3

Ruth descends the stairs, pours a glass of white wine she'd been chilling in the kitchen refrigerator, and phones a number in Memphis.

"Aunt Katherine, I'm in Brevard, looking through some old family files. It's been an interesting afternoon. But I have a question. Who in the world is Eulie?"

Bolivar, TN, 1927

Eulie hears birdsong, a Carolina wren, she thinks. She doesn't remember what day it is. She has no idea where she is. The words *"Why am I not in Memphis?"* form in her mind, then vanish.

She stares at the ceiling in the mostly dark room and traces the outline of a single bare lightbulb with her moving eyes until it resembles an inverted question mark and then a dangling hook that might suspend one of her mother's dresses. She thinks of a man she dated, Jim, and wonders why he doesn't want to marry her. Why he stopped calling. Why he's not here.

Her eyes close and slowly open. A repeated rhythm that calms her along with breaths she begins to count. Several minutes pass. The birds startle and fly away. Silence and wind now occupy her thoughts.

Eulie looks up at the high shelf in dim light, just after dawn, and sees the suitcase she received from her parents on the day she graduated from high school, the same suitcase she took to SMU (Southern Methodist University) on the train for journalism school. The suitcase is out of reach, even if she could stand on the bed, but standing is not even a possibility in her mind. She wiggles her fingers, and then slowly flexes her ankles. Both actions require concentration and immense energy, friction against the straps.

She barely makes out her name and address on the luggage tag. With the help of a rubber band, another larger rectangle of cardboard dangles from the handle. The larger tag is easier to read—ATTIC 4.

Eulie wonders about the contents of her suitcase and tries to remember, shaking her head quickly several times, the memory too much to think about right now. Brief and fast images—a medicine bottle, broken glass, bloody gauze, her father holding a handful of pills—flash across her mind. Water flowing from the faucet in the bathroom, pooling in the sink.

She breathes and slowly counts. Her eyes remain open. What is this place? What year is this? How did I get here?

A gentle, clear voice that doesn't sound real, disembodied, calls down a corridor, maybe a tunnel. "It's 7 a.m., Tuesday morning."

Eulie doesn't recognize the voice and cannot locate its source either in the morning air or maybe in her mind. Same voice, same words, twice more.

A key enters a lock. A bolt softly slides and stops. A door opens.

"It's time for breakfast, Miss Ewell," the same voice reports. "I'll be back shortly and help you get dressed."

Eulie turns her head on the pillow, first toward the window and then the open door. She squints as if searching a wide landscape over a long distance.

"No one has called me by that name in a very long time," she whispers.

Chattanooga, TN, Fall 1974

Ruth is on the phone with a man who is asking dozens of questions.

"Yes, her niece."

"No, I've never met her, never seen her."

"My father died just over a year ago. I'm the oldest of his three daughters. No one ever told us about her."

"She was born in Arkansas in 1902. Probably listed as Ewell in your records."

"My mother is in a nursing facility here in this city."

"A few old photos in an attic file cabinet."

"What do I have to do to gain access to her medical records? How long would that take?"

"My aunt Katherine still lives in Memphis and used to schedule occasional visits with Eulie, her sister, for many years, but she no longer drives."

"Yes, *prefrontal lobotomy*. Those are the words Aunt Katherine used. And I know these were once performed at Bolivar."

"I do plan on visiting soon. Who . . . whom should I contact and what time of day would be best?"

Bolivar, TN, 1928

Eulie takes a seat in the large dining hall with fourteen widely spaced tables (she counted—four, five, another five), six chairs at each table. The tables are marked with large numbers in a clasp atop a narrow stand like those in a restaurant, marking where menu orders should be delivered, except each table already has food, all plates the same, one spoon on each napkin. No fork, no knife.

Wheelchairs dot the hall at the ends of some tables, rolled in last after everyone else is seated. All females for this meal-shift; several of the residents do not raise their heads—chin on chest, eyes closed—when the voice (slow, measured, and clear) comes over an intercom.

"Good morning, ladies. It's 7:45 in the beautiful state of Tennessee. The Tuesday schedule is under your plate. You have thirty minutes to enjoy your food before the men's wings start to arrive. Take your time. Eat a good, healthy breakfast. Then you can return to your rooms until nine. Have a good day here in Bolivar. It's presently 38 degrees outside with a high expected of 57 under sunny March skies. Spring is on the way."

A small bird flies back and forth several times across the large room before resting on a high ceiling rafter. Eulie watches it, perched, for at least a minute until an attendant tells her that the eggs will soon be cold unless she eats them. The same attendant helps Eulie tuck the cloth napkin under her chin.

Eulie looks at the food on her plate but is mostly wondering about the bird, how it got inside and how it's maybe trapped and unable to fly out. She raises her eyes to the ceiling, looks right and left, slowly, but cannot find the bird.

She closes her eyes and thinks about praying because nobody else did. From a backseat, she sees her parents in the front, her father driving a car. Her mother turns around and smiles with wet eyes.

The food is cold, but she's hungry and eats all of it—eggs, toast and jam, grits with pooled melted butter, two sausage patties best eaten with fingers. Thirsty, she drinks the orange juice in three long swallows. She notices grease lines smudging the glass and thinks about her job busing tables to help with expenses at college.

Eulie finishes her breakfast before anyone else at her table. One older woman with long gray hair, tied behind her neck in a ponytail, has not started, not a bite. The woman catches Eulie's stare, bares her clenched teeth, and emits a low, almost inaudible growl.

No one speaks—only the soft clinking of spoons and sipping—until a woman three tables down moans, rocking back and forth, then screams. Eulie, startled, notices the bird again flying around the room.

The sun throws bright light on the lower quarter of the room where no one is sitting, reflecting off the waxed wooden floor.

CHAPTER 3

Memphis, Interstate 40, Winter 1975

They enter four-lane traffic, thinned from morning rush hour, and head east on a Tuesday in January. The forecast calls for a chance of snow in the metro area, but not until later that afternoon. A bright glare on the horizon causes Ruth to reach across her aunt Katherine, retrieving sunglasses from the Buick's glove compartment.

She spent last night at her aunt's condo in the city after driving alone for six hours, skirting just south of Nashville on the interstate. Ruth fights back a yawn. They'd stayed up late. Talking, laughing, and crying with various degrees of intensity.

"I'm still not sure why all of you, my entire family, chose to hide her from us. I thought about it all through the drive from Chattanooga, wondered about the long collaborative secrecy in bed last night, looking up at the dark ceiling. *Why?*"

It's easier, Ruth finds, to pose such candid questions from behind the safety of dark glasses. A long silence settles between them as they exit the interstate toward Bolivar.

Katherine looks out the window, choosing her words carefully. She speaks as Ruth looks straight ahead, short gaps of time after each measured sentence.

"Your father wasn't long back from the war—horrible fighting, gas masks in the Black Forest, still dealing with bad dreams just before he married your mom in Georgia and they moved to Brevard. Eulie's breakdown around that time just seemed like it was too much to talk about, too much to even think about, coupled with the horror your father experienced. I don't know what else to say, really, other than what we shared last night. I'm sorry, Ruthie. Family secrets, I've learned, are never a good idea. I feel like I've betrayed my favorite niece."

The sun continues to rise, now behind thick cloud cover. Ruth removes the sunglasses and tosses them on the dashboard. They slide across the vinyl on a sharp bend in the two-lane road, landing at Katherine's feet, breaking the silence. Both women look at one another and smile.

"I do love you, Auntie K. Always have. You've always seemed like the sane one in the family. You know how father could get, retreating to his gin and all the books upstairs. And whatever he was squirreling away in the attic. I do appreciate you helping me gain access to the medical records. You've seen them at some point, yes?"

"I know most of what happened. The invasive brain surgery, the shock therapy, then various drug treatments. She was so hard to handle at times—heard voices, saw visions, rambling disconnected speeches, and occasional angry accusations. Probably what scared away the man she was dating after returning from SMU, early signs of her illness then, don't you think?"

"Undoubtedly."

"I sometimes wonder why my parents, your grandparents, didn't ask more about such extreme measures. And I sometimes wonder if they were just experimenting on her and others. The lobotomy, believe it or not, actually helped her symptoms for a while but then later seemed to make everything even worse. You spent that whole summer in Memphis with them as a teenager. It was 1947, I think? I was living elsewhere at the time before we moved back to the city. And do recall hearing how much you loved those months. I know they never spoke of her to you, but you saw no photos of Eulie around the house that summer? No evidence of another daughter?"

"No, nothing. I was only a few miles away from her then and didn't know it."

"Your grandparents did travel often to Bolivar at first."

"And you?"

"Yes, at first. Before the surgery. The visits from all of us became more infrequent after her relapse. It was so hard to see her, almost impossible to converse, meaningfully. That's no excuse, however. I did go maybe three times per year. I feel a lot of shame from not seeing my sister more."

"Will she recognize you today?"

"Maybe. Probably on some level. We left photos in her room, but they're old now. An attendant told me that she does look at them sometimes. I'm sort of afraid to replace them with more updated faces. I don't know if that would be disturbing for her, or if whatever memories she once had of us would then be gone, or maybe confused."

They stopped for an early lunch at a diner in Whiteville, looking out the window near their table at people walking on the sidewalk, mostly eating in silence.

A light snow was falling as they returned to the car. Twenty minutes later, Katherine points to a sign: WESTERN STATE HOSPITAL. The word "welcome" on the sign seemed out of place but understandable to Ruth, who says so.

The niece turns down a long driveway, past a row of tall oak trees, several large branches on the ground from recent wind that raged through the western part of the state, barreling up through the tip of Kentucky and on toward the Ohio Valley.

She parks and both women don heavy coats before exiting the car. Ruth takes her aunt's gloved hand. They walk toward the four-story building and stop for a moment, looking up at the falling snow through the dark fingers of the tall trees.

Under the steep eaves, near the roof, a woman in a robe stands at what must be an attic room window and waves through thin iron bars. Several birds fly from the roof toward an open field.

"That's not Eulie," Katherine says.

Bolivar, TN, 1943

An attendant, a tall smiling man named Jack, arrives at room number four, the next-to-last room in the short attic hallway, renovated due to lack of space just under twenty years ago.

"Miss Ewell, it's time to go downstairs now."

With assistance, Eulie stands beside her bed. She's forty-one, but looks older—long uncombed dark hair, three missing teeth, sallow complexion, unfocused eyes that dart around the room. In her open palm Jack places two orange oval tablets; they are ingested with a glass of water without complaint.

She is wearing a surgical gown, tied loosely at the back. Jack helps her onto the long gurney in a sitting position. He tells her where they're going, how this procedure will help her feel better, a bit about what the room will look like, feel like, descriptions of today's weather—a warm springtime day in April, just after Easter—and how the children hunted colored eggs recently at a nearby church he attends. All of this meant to soothe Eulie but also to bide time as the sedative settles in.

Eulie's eyes, drooping, open and close. Jack slowly lowers her into a reclining position, straps securing arms and feet. She sees a dark suitcase on an upper shelf just before closing her eyes and falling asleep. They exit the room with a careful left turn and make their way down the hallway to an elevator. Jack types in a code and they begin a slow descent to the basement.

Eulie is dreaming. She dreams of a long swing in her childhood front yard in Texarkana. Brother pushing her, both laughing. Sister walking across the lawn with a tray of lemonade. Mother is on the porch snapping beans, pulling the curling strings from each narrow spine, occasionally calling instructions for the children to be careful.

Higher she climbs in the swing, Brother laughing harder as his pushes intensify. At the apex of her rearward swing, Eulie sees a nest in the branches with three small eggs. Twice she sees the nest. And then two birds perched nearby in the upper branches. *Maybe the parents*, she thinks.

The elevator opens for the basement floor. Jack guides the gurney down a long hall under dim, precisely spaced ceiling lights, through two sets of double doors. They turn right into a bright room.

In her mind, Eulie squints through the branches of the tree at the bright sun that's emerged from behind a cloud.

Two men and two women, each gowned in white, surround Eulie. She opens her eyes, smiling, and then shakes her head quickly, at first mistaking the group for members of her family. Before entering again into a deep sleep, she wonders if she's in heaven with them.

Forest Hill Funeral Home, Memphis, 1989

Katherine takes Ruth's hand.

They walk to the front of the small chapel where an open casket rests at the end of the middle aisle. A spray of roses rests upon the lower half of "her soft wooden bed," a phrase used by the funeral home director that Ruth secretly detests.

The two women are alone for now. Other family members, four they think, will arrive in the next half hour with the Methodist minister from Katherine's church, a young man not long out of seminary.

An electronic organ is off to the right, a bit above them, but there will be no hymns, no music. "Eulie did not like music," Katherine whispers, even though there's no need to be quiet. "Not after her surgery."

They stop at the edge of the casket, still holding hands. At least a minute passes, both women crying without words.

"Her hair was always beautiful," Katherine says. "Never turned white."

Ruth hugs her aunt. And touches her other aunt in the casket, allowing her hand to rest there while she prays in silence.

Several weeks from now, the niece from Chattanooga will tell Katherine what she's discovered. That mental illness, she suspects, has been the genetic, sad legacy in their family for a very long time. That she's worried for her own sons, her own future.

Words for another day, she thinks, holding Katherine.

Not this one.

Dallas, TX, June 1925

A young woman makes her way up the narrow aisle of the evening train. The fourth passenger car is only half full. She has plenty of room to stow her suitcase on the iron slats above her head, secured with canvas straps to prevent jostling on the many stops, including Texarkana, between here and Memphis.

Eulie smiles, conjuring pleasant memories of her childhood, but knows the small town will be too dark by the time the train passes through to notice much. Maybe she'll see the bare outline of the ridge on the north side where she grew up and played with siblings in neighborhood woods that they called a forest.

She notices the conductor waving to a train steward on the outside platform, arranges a small pillow next to the window, and retrieves a book from her purse—a short biography of Benjamin Franklin, sent by her brother to the freshman dorm at SMU.

According to her ticket, the train should depart the station in two minutes at 7:56 p.m. She will arrive in Memphis just after dawn, plenty of time to sleep, perhaps arriving fresh for her parents, who'll be waiting on her train with Katherine and the family car, ready to take her home at last to the room she once shared with her sister.

She laughs softly, smiling, thinking of the plans for tomorrow evening in their backyard. A reunion party that will include her favorite cake and also her boyfriend, Jim, whose recent letters to Texas surprised her with unexpected, gentlemanly romantic intensity.

The train pulls away from the station and slowly gathers speed. It's early June, a warm evening. Eulie watches children swing and teeter-totter in a city playground with their parents talking nearby in a cluster. She looks back at the Dallas skyline as the sun begins to set behind the tallest buildings.

Eyes open, Eulie offers a silent prayer thanking God for helping her with final semester exams and the last of the term papers.

She looks again at her reflection in the window glass. Lips are moving in the reflection with some sort of message. She touches her mouth. Her lips are still. The reflection keeps talking.

Eulie closes her eyes and shakes her head again, not for the first time that week. Not for the first time that semester. With the rocking train, she sleeps. And will sleep all night until the train arrives in Memphis.

*

I did a good bit of reading and research before writing the short story. I gathered information concerning the Tennessee state hospital in Bolivar (part of which is still operational) and viewed recent photos of its rather eerie and abandoned hallways.[1] I devoured a book about the history of lobotomies in the middle part of the twentieth century and how the famous "icepick" procedure (developed by Dr. Walter Freeman) and related electroshock therapies actually helped some patients with severe psychotic symptoms, at least temporarily, but largely rendered many recipients (including my aunt Eulie, apparently) in a more comatose and less communicative state.[2] I read William Styron's classic reflection on his own bouts with depression, *Darkness Visible* (1992), and Kay Redfield Jamison's fascinating memoir, *An Unquiet Mind: A Memoir of Moods and Madness* (1995).[3] And many other articles and essays related to schizophrenia, mood disorders, and the rather bleak history of mental health care in the United States.[4]

I even probed the bizarre life of Georgia Tann, a social worker in nearby Memphis (only seventy miles from Bolivar) who sold over five thousand children into adoption under the lucrative and demented guise of "helping" their birth mothers. Tann had easy access to Western State Hospital and other Tennessee institutions. For nearly thirty years (spanning the time Eulie was a resident), all babies born at Western State were sent to Tann's adoption agency. Some of the children became underage farmhands across the United States and in England. Others were adopted by wealthy celebrities on the West Coast.

There is no historical evidence that my aunt Eulie was pregnant at the time of her first breakdown, but the proximity of her mental health problems at SMU to the sudden ending of a relationship with a man to whom she was almost engaged intrigued me. Was Eulie possibly pregnant when she entered Bolivar? Could she have met Georgia Tann?

In early July of 2024, I placed a call to the records department of the hospital in Bolivar and spoke to a very friendly and helpful woman named Jenny. As we spoke, I envisioned Jenny in a vast dimly lit basement with records dating back to the late 1800s when the hospital was built and received its first residents.

I'd been putting off this phone call. My mother had gained access to Eulie's records, seven years after her aunt's death. I knew some details about Eulie's stay in Bolivar, over fifty years as a state hospital resident. Mom included a rather cryptic footnote in her genealogy binder, *A Search for Yesterday*, the gift she left to her three sons: "In 1996, I obtained a court order to open Ewell's medical records. Her records are private information and shall remain so."

Mom died in June of 2017. My father died nine months later, mostly of deep grief. Before either died, my younger brother, Lee, a college professor living in Washington State, was diagnosed with a brain cancer known as glioblastoma, a slow-developing and incurable cancer, treatment of which gave its victims only a bit of time, rarely over three years. I was visiting my parents one Sunday afternoon in their residential facility near my home and found my father crying. He was upset that his youngest son might precede him in death. "It's just not the proper order of things," my weepy dad lamented.

"Well, we can always arrange to have you killed first, Bob," said my mother, darkly—shaped by a form of dementia, according to her neurologist, that often removed the editorial "screen" from her brainwaves—in a fashion that strangely made us all laugh, even through the tears.

Knowing my mother and her odd slant on the world, I concluded that her cryptic footnote about "Ewell's medical records" was basically a posthumous invitation to look further on our own if we wanted more information about Eulie's past.

Jenny was on the other end of the phone line, listening to my halting reason for calling. Before dialing the number in Bolivar, I rehearsed the reasons I did indeed want to know more—human curiosity; William Styron's own journey from embarrassment for his condition to making his own "darkness visible" in a way that was liberating and inspiring; and several mental health challenges occurring with Eulie's immediate descendants, suggesting a clear genetic link in my mother's side of the family going back untold generations and passed on with various intensities to my brother, my aunt, a cousin, and yours truly.

I explained to Jenny why I was calling. She patiently described the process and said at one point that "we need a court order from the state of Tennessee," something that wasn't that difficult to obtain if I could provide proof of relation. This was all doable, I thought. I was so glad my hesitancy to call hadn't won out.

"I forgot to ask," Jenny suddenly mentioned, "about the year of your great-aunt's death. It's a state law that we destroy all patient records ten years after a resident is deceased."

*

I wrote a short story in 2019, "Pastor Polar," that won first place in fiction in the annual Porter Fleming Literary Competition, a regional contest fielding entries from twelve southern states and sponsored by the Morris Museum of Art in Augusta, Georgia. The award came with a very nice cash prize and an invitation to read the story that spring at the museum as the final round of the Masters golf classic was played nearby.

The story recounts a single alarming and unraveling day in the life of an unnamed bipolar pastor who has forgotten to take his daily medication. This tale is decidedly fictional (and I had a great time writing it), but this opening section describes me at times:

> *5:07 AM.* I've just completed my weight lifting routine in the garage (early these summer days to beat the heat) with an eighty-pound bar and precisely 115 bench repetitions in descending clusters of twenty, fifteen, and ten. That's 9,200 pounds every other morning.
>
> Now a battery of stretches on the living room floor including a yoga pose known as "the horse," involving opposite arm and leg extremities, balancing on one knee. Our cat, Portia, sometimes joins me. It's amusing to observe how her front and back paws extend to mimic my own stretch—a cat doing the horse.
>
> Water bubbles in an early boil on the stove. Conserving energy, I turn off the eye. Upon stepping out of the shower the egg will be ready for me to peel. I detest wasting time. Several things can usually be accomplished at once with a little forethought. People could get so much more done in a day if they only stopped to plan and ponder. Sadly, most wait for the day to come to them. . . . I tease my wife and children and tell them I can "see the future," but any high school graduate should be able to control most of the day by using their God-given senses and adhering to what I call "Consequence Theology," the unfailing maxim that certain consequences always follow certain behaviors in a repeated pattern as obvious and expected as gravity.[5]

The pastor in this manic tale is not intended to be me. He mocks a secretarial candidate in a morning interview, is booked by a surprised policeman that afternoon, concocts a dazzling excuse covering his tardiness for incredulous church council members at their evening meeting, forgets his wife's birthday, and discovers just before midnight that his church has canned him.

None of that has happened to me, thankfully. But I was able to write the story partly due to my own challenges, going on almost forty years now, with what my physician has called "mild bipolarity"—an inherited illness, I'm convinced. An illness that allows me to sometimes get a lot done in a given day—I once wrote a short book on sanctification, a Lutheran best seller, in a two-week period (just sayin')—but also an illness with accompanying behavior that my wife has occasionally described as "asshole-ish." That's the (usually mild) manic swing kicking in. But then the inevitable polar descent: the creative and utterly pleasurable manic intensity followed by the predictable period of dark depression.

With the exception of two weeks-long periods of bleak darkness (recalling William Styron) at ages thirty and fifty-two, the illness has been controlled with a daily dose of lithium, #3 on the periodic table of elements, whose pharmacological benefits were not widely known in America (nor was the drug prescribed) until the late 1950s. My polar ups and downs have been largely (and blessedly) controlled with a natural element as innocuous as table salt. I liken lithium in my life to a daily vitamin without which I could careen in unhealthy directions. Other sufferers with bipolarity have not been so fortunate. Kay Redfield Jamison (whose work, as I've noted, is a heavenly gift on the subject) has lived through a virtual minefield of erratic behaviors, including jumping out of a moving car in her twenties, feeling invincible. She writes: "I have become fundamentally and deeply skeptical that anyone who does not have this illness can truly understand it. . . . *No* amount of love can cure madness or unblacken one's dark moods. Love can help, it can make the pain more tolerable, but, always, one is beholden to medication that may or may not always work and may or may not be bearable."[6]

It took me a long time to decide to write openly about my illness for this book. We've made huge national headway in this regard, but an immense amount of stigma and shame still surrounds disorders affecting mental cognition (depression, dementia, anxiety, to name only three), which, by some estimates, affects up to 50 percent of the general population at some point in their lives. It also took me a long time (years) to admit that the illness was something I could not control without help. Part of this liberating insight was connected to genealogical discoveries I kept coming across and the eventual self-admission that I had no more control over my inherited family chemistry than I had over my height or the color of my hair.

There is still a lot of embarrassment surrounding illnesses of the brain that contributes to (often avoidable) erratic and alarming behaviors. And a lot of hiding. My aunt Eulie was hidden away (even from members of her own family) for over half a century with schizophrenia, a malady that's different but unquestionably related to bipolar illness.[7]

Has God been intentionally acting through such wounded genealogies? Or is inherited illness (the main topic of this chapter) just a sad luck of the draw?

*

The psalms are full of (rather transparent) mood swings described throughout a corpus of 150 prayers. Here are just a few:

> For you strike all my enemies on the cheek;
> you break the teeth of the wicked. (3:7)

> I am weary with my moaning;
> every night I flood my bed with tears. (6:6)

> Break the arm of the wicked and evildoers. (10:15)

> By my God I can leap over a wall. (18:29)

Turn to me and be gracious to me,
    for I am lonely and afflicted. (25:16)

You have turned my mourning into dancing. (30:11)

The LORD is near to the brokenhearted,
    and saves the crushed in spirit. (34:18)

O Lord, all my longing is known to you;
    my sighing is not hidden from you. (38:9)

    Do not hold your peace at my tears.
For I am your passing guest,
    an alien, like all my forebears. (39:12)

Rouse yourself! Why do you sleep, O Lord? (44:23)

You have kept count of my tossings;
    put my tears in your bottle. (56:8)

Let [my enemies] be like the snail that dissolves into
    slime. (58:8)

For the human heart and mind are deep. (64:6)

You have fed your people with the bread of tears,
    and given them tears to drink in full measure.
    (80:5)

Pursue them with your tempest
    and terrify them with your hurricane. (83:15)

I lie awake;
    I am like a lonely bird on the housetop. (102:7)

He will execute judgment . . . ;
he will shatter heads over the wide earth. (110:6)

Their hearts are fat and gross. (119:70)

Scholars disagree concerning how many of the psalms were actually written by David. But almost all psalm savants concur that he wrote at least half of them. Recalling the impressive list of female heroes in Jesus's genealogy, we should not forget that King David also plays an important and vital role in the Messiah's genetic inheritance as the Lord's great-great- (and then some) granddaddy whose feats of faith and wisdom surely shape the exploits of one sent to save the world.

This is only a small slice of many psalms featuring a vast array of emotions, but I find it striking that David's transparent prayers are filled with enough instances of sadness, elation, suspicion, anxiety, and mood swings to make me wonder whether he also might have benefited from a daily dose of mind-soothing medication.[8]

David's bed is regularly full of tears. He employs colorful language that probably could have benefited from an editor. He offers thoughts of invincibility. He prays that God might knock out the teeth of his enemies, break their arms, and terrify them with category 5 storms; that he would shatter the heads of the unjust. The last image conjures God as the Ultimate Good Guy in a WWE tag-team wrestling match in a ring filled with evil despots who are "fat and gross."

I like these prayers. They present a definite green light inviting the full gamut of human emotion to the Lord in prayer. But they also reveal that David is a messy stew of thoughts through whom God works and consistently chooses. These traits are not random aspects of David's overall personality but instead reveal a man whom God chooses, guides, and redeems in spite of his flaws. It's impossible to understand the providential nature of God's choice of David by airbrushing parts of his complicated personality from the genealogical inheritance he would pass on to those who followed him generationally.

Kay Redfield Jamison has pondered whether she'd choose another life without the bizarre unpredictability of bipolar illness if given the chance. Despite the consistent burdens of the illness, she's quick to note its plus side: "So why would I want anything to do with this illness? Because I honestly believe that as a result of it I have felt more things, more deeply; had more experiences, more intensely; loved more, and been more loved; laughed more often for having cried more often; appreciated more the springs, for all the winters. . . . But, normal or manic, I have run faster, thought faster, and loved faster than most I know. And I think much of this is related to my illness—the intensity it gives to things and the perspective it forces on me."[9]

Even though Jamison never suggests that God is helping her cope with its downside or is responsible for the good things that have come out of her illness, she acknowledges its gifts and refuses a hypothetical opportunity to remove its negative effects. Others, I suspect, with a different inherited illness would indeed change or alter the very challenging lives they lead if offered an alternative.

Elyn Saks, who suffers with schizophrenia, ponders such a possibility after fielding a question lovingly posed by a friend: "If there were a pill that would instantly cure me, would I take it?" Saks notes the risks of such a startling change in her life, also acknowledging her gifts, and quotes the poet Rainer Maria Rilke, who said, "Don't take away my devils because my angels may flee too."

But Saks returns to the possibility: "My psychosis is a waking nightmare, in which my demons are so terrifying that all my angels have already fled. So would I take the pill? In a heartbeat."[10]

Billy Joel, the singer and songwriter, has talked about his own struggles with bipolar illness and its place in his music and creative life. His powerful song "Summer, Highland Falls" (one of my favorites) describes a life of "either sadness or euphoria," polarities that both gift and plague a variety of artists and writers. The high and the fall alluded to in Joel's song title undoubtedly fuel creative energy for him even amid the lows. I doubt Joel would change his life if invited to consider another.

I wonder, however, if the same could be said of Pastor Maltbie Babcock, who wrote the beautiful and much-loved hymn "This Is My Father's World," with its memorable and upbeat lyrics celebrating God's creation. Maltbie asks in the hymn, "Why should my heart be sad?" given "the morning light, the lily white" and all nature singing in concert with "the music of the spheres." Surely a hymn on the top ten list of most any Christian denomination.

But Pastor Babcock was indeed intermittently sad. I recently learned that he suffered from depression and committed suicide in 1901 at the age of forty-two.

✶

Does the Bible offer a theological response to the reality of inherited illness passed on through the decades in a long march of genealogical time?

As someone who has definitely dealt with the pluses and minuses of nameable genetic inheritance, I sometimes think of Saint Paul's marvelous and strange description of "a person in Christ who fourteen years ago was caught up to the third heaven . . . and heard things that are not to be told, that no mortal is permitted to repeat" (2 Cor. 12:2, 4). Given that prohibitive caveat, Paul repeats a colorful chunk of the testimony anyway. He reveals this odd witness as if it happened to a close friend in a rather bizarre celestial up-and-back. Most scholars, however, believe that our prolific letter writer is describing an event that he actually experienced fourteen years prior to the penning of this correspondence to parishioners who might have raised an eyebrow or two had Paul claimed the experience as his own. "Whether in the body or out of the body I do not know, God knows." Twice Paul says this

(12:2 and 12:3) of the vividly described paranormal travel odyssey. The congregation might be thinking: *Whether in his mind or out of it, we're not sure.*

Why not come right out and claim the experience as Paul's own? Possibly because of some version of the stigma (then and now) that is attached to the claiming of such odd events.

There has always been a certain (but reserved) fascination with Christian practices that border on hokum and flirt with the bizarre. For example, during one of our moves to a new parish, my wife, Cindy (unbeknownst to me), buried a small statue of Saint Joseph in the front yard, upside down, facing the house—a fairly common practice, I'm told, that's supposed to help the house sell quickly. A tradition, however, that might leave Martin Luther spinning in his grave. I later asked Cindy why she didn't just go straight to the top and bury Jesus himself in the front yard.

I suspect that the first listeners to Paul's letter were familiar with such strange practices and testimonies,[11] but he surely knew there were audience credibility limits. Safer, I suppose, to describe his experience as if it occurred to someone else.

Later in the same passage, Paul reveals some personal information that fascinates me. Noting the "exceptional character of the revelations" (12:7), and thus cementing in my own mind that he's describing his own past and not someone else's, Paul describes "a thorn . . . in the flesh" that was given to him to "keep [him] from being too elated" (12:7). The phrase concerning elation is mentioned twice. And an appeal to the Lord for the thorn to be removed occurs, prayerfully, thrice.

The exact nature of this "thorn" that bugged the dickens out of Paul is never specifically described. The connection between "elation" and accompanying affliction intrigues me. If Paul was indeed suffering from some version of bipolar illness—the psychological swings between elated insight and depression—this might indeed explain his periods of extreme creativity and energy that at times seemed able to overcome incredible obstacles and intense opposition to his fiery missional work. It would also explain the downhearted tenor that often seeps through his transparent writing style.

Paul prays about his "thorn." He wants to be rid of it. The Lord responds. "He said to me, 'My grace is sufficient for you, for power is made perfect in weakness.' So, I will boast all the more gladly of my weaknesses, so that the power of Christ may dwell in me. Therefore I am content with weaknesses, insults, hardships, persecutions, and calamities for the sake of Christ; for whenever I am weak, then I am strong" (2 Cor. 12:9–10). These are remarkable and rather shocking claims in any century, comments that do not sell well in Peoria or anywhere else. They will not be taken seriously in halls of power where national decisions are made. The words make little sense in cancer wards or divorce courts or refugee camps.

And I suspect these assertions are not all that comforting for people who ponder the nature of an inherited illness. "A thorn was given me in the flesh," says Paul, who repeatedly prays for its removal. Perhaps you've prayed many more times than that for your own thorny situation. Add to your theological ponderings the recollection that Jesus wore a crown of thorns on that Friday afternoon long ago, mockingly affixed to his head. There is veiled power in such weakness and such wounds, but often in hiding for most of us; this is utterly paradoxical.

In a related passage from Paul's pen, written to the same group of Christians and revealing the cross as the hidden power of God (1 Cor. 1:18): "God chose what is foolish in the world to shame the wise; God chose what is weak in the world to shame the strong; God chose what is low and despised in the world, things that are not, to reduce to nothing things that are, so that no one might boast in the presence of God" (1 Cor. 1:27–29).

When I was preaching every Sunday, this passage from the lectionary appeared in the Epiphany season, usually on Super Bowl Sunday. I once pointed out during a sermon (revealing the "power" imbalance that day) that God's first-round draft choices of the foolish, weak, low, and despised would get absolutely creamed by the Denver Broncos. *Two bits, four bits, six bits, a dollar, all for crucifixion, stand up and holler!*

But I have seen the truth in Paul's unusual claim in my own complicated genetic inheritance (and in other thorny lives), leading to a sincere mistrust of religious elation as the primary litmus test of true faithfulness. Christians are handed body and blood each Sunday morning, after all, not sunshine and cookies. There is indeed a veiled power here, a kind of unbreakable thorny strength that God forms in people over time. The Greek word that Paul uses for "thorn," by the way, is *skolops*, a word suggesting a sharp stake involving impalement, conjuring images of other wounds endured by a well-known sufferer.

*

The disciples were together on that first Easter evening, hiding behind locked doors. I don't blame them. Crucifixions were contagious. Suddenly Jesus stands among them and says, "Peace be with you" (John 20:19).

Then he raises his tunic and points to the recent wound on his side; pulls back sleeves and invites a close gander at his palms. "*Then* the disciples rejoiced when they saw the Lord" (20:20). And not a second sooner. It's an important Easter detail.

Near the end of *The Odyssey*, Homer's ancient tale, Odysseus finally returns home. Many years have passed from a long journey. The family nurse, Eurycleia, begins to bathe a man whom she thinks is some stranger. Only when she sees Odysseus's old hunting wound does recognition occur. From book 19 of the old epic: "This was the scar the old nurse recognized; she traced it under her spread hands, then let it go, and into the basin fell the lower leg. . . . Her eyes filled up with tears; her throat closed, and she whispered, 'Oh yes! *You are Odysseus!* Ah, dear child! I could not see you until now.'"

Jesus showed them his wounds. Twice he connects these scars to his offering of peace. The disciples rejoiced when they saw their old friend. They could not see him until then. "*As* the Father has sent me, so I send you" (20:21). A small word with only two letters but filled with enormous possibility for church life where we're used to hiding our scars, or being embarrassed by them.

This ancient Easter evening reunion suggests a vital purpose for congregations usually filled with various people struggling with some version of an inherited illness. One test of faithful community is to follow Jesus's lead here. How will church members safely reveal their wounds to one another? Present scars that have perhaps led to isolation and shaken faith? How will a church community be sent into the world "as" the Father once sent Jesus?

Far more than assembling with relative strangers for an hour each week, church unites us in community with precisely what we have in common—not our potential, or social standing, or even our shared Lutheran theology, but centrally our scars and how Jesus forms and calls a congregation to discover and help bear the wounds of others.

So he stands in the middle of the community, with palms outstretched, wounds wide open for examination. "Peace be with you," says Jesus. And when *we* share this peace with each other before Holy Communion each week, it's far more than a way of saying, "Good morning, so good to see you. How about those Clemson Tigers?" (Or insert your favorite sports team.)

The liturgical practice of "sharing the peace" resurfaced in most Lutheran congregations with the advent of *The Lutheran Book of Worship* (1978), but stretches much further back to the first decades of the early church. In this ancient worship gesture we offer profound hope and reconciliation, daring to share life's agonies and joys. Afterward, the church passes around body and blood. Again, please ponder the implications of such an earthy exchange.

Jesus exhibited scars even on Easter. And so we come to terms with our own—a large part of anyone's identity. As we share old and fresh wounds safely in community, perhaps Christ is saying to us: "Ah, dear children. I could not see you. I could not see you until now."

The body of Christ, apparently, is most visible when our scars are revealed.

*

Heidi Haverkamp writes, "To say 'I don't know' as a prayer, confession, or meditation is not to give up but to witness to the gap of unknowing between us and God. A gap not of cold emptiness but of wonder; a gap where there is more space for relating to one another and a clearing for the path that leads us back again to the mystery and glory of God."[12]

I understand the strong desire to discover one's genetic inheritance. I understand the need to spit in a small container and mail part of yourself away, waiting in anticipation on the revealed data. I understand the desire to search and glean insight into the past, an attempt to connect to unknown forebears and perhaps learn more about one's own peculiar proclivities, health realities, and habits. There is, however, much we can never know, a holy and mysterious gap between revealed data and a deity who "searches and knows" us all (Ps. 139:1). There are many opportunities for prayer and wonder within the territory of that unknown and permanent gap.

My aunt Eulie was hidden and invisible to many of her family members for many years. With her medical records now gone, there is much I'll never know. But when I think of her in that Tennessee state hospital, I still wonder what her days must have been like, what sort of care she received, what the personalities of the hospital staff were like, how the hospital was surely filled with caring people who hopefully did the best they could given the limited knowledge of the day.

In her Pulitzer Prize–winning novel *Night Watch*, Jayne Anne Phillips uses the Trans-Allegheny Lunatic Asylum in West Virginia for much of the book's setting, a facility modeled on the groundbreaking and compassionate work of Quaker physician Thomas Story Kirkbride (1809–1883), whose "moral treatment" of the mentally ill influenced the architecture of many asylums in the United States during the nineteenth century, including Western State Hospital near Memphis, where Eulie spent much of her life. This passage from Phillips's novel describes the first view of the asylum, early one morning after several days of travel by wagon, for a new resident and a caring daughter who has accompanied her troubled mother just after the Civil War:

> The broad gravel path of the entrance led far back to the castle, and the stone walls, four or five stories high, went off to both sides as far as I could see. Straight paths crisscrossed the grounds but the widest one led to the huge front doors. There was a circle halfway on, with a fountain and round pool in the middle, and benches arranged around it. Then the path led to the stone steps and arched doors of the building. It looked as though there would be many doors, for the long wings and many windows, with cupolas topping the roof, but there was just one door, bigger than any I'd seen, with oval leaded glass windows on each side, and a leaded glass pyramid for a transom window. A wide palace door for a prince or princess. All was silent.[13]

Soon to enter my seventies, I do think that God has led me to a late interest in Eulie, not only because of my own genetic inheritance but also as a response to the God who created me and still searches for me, searches for us all who are "fearfully and wonderfully made" (Ps. 139:14).

Fear and wonder indeed describe the gap of unknowing in these genealogical matters reasonably well, yielding eventually to prayer. I'll never know what Eulie thought, or much of what she might have experienced on a daily basis. I do know that she's part of me, a contributor to a complicated mind that's able to write books and deliver effective sermons but is also occasionally plagued with dark moods, helped with medicine that would surely have helped her had it been available. That Eulie was a journalism major at SMU, interested in writing, connects our two lives all the more. My days are undeniably shaped by a complicated genetic inheritance. I suspect that's overwhelmingly true for many who've yet to begin a search.

Inherited illness shapes my daily life and my worldview. But what about inherited incident? Do rather bleak incidents from the distant past, buried in my genealogy long before my birth, speak to the days I'm now living?

Chapter 4

GENEALOGY AND INHERITED INCIDENT

"But I am holding half an acre
Torn from the map of Michigan
I am carrying this scrap of paper
That can crack the darkest sky wide open."

—From "Half Acre" by the musical ensemble Hem

"Keep us all in grace, and guide us when perplexed, and free us from all harm in this world and the next."

—Martin Rinkhart (1586–1649), "Now Thank We All Our God"

I've lived just over sixty-seven years on the planet in the states of Tennessee, South Carolina, North Carolina, and Virginia. One move involved college, the others were born of pastoral call in four diverse settings ranging between open farmland, urban sidewalks, and relative small-town insularity, each context filled with fascinating characters and unforgettable stories. The South is a region brimming with odd stories and famous writers, absolutely dripping in tales of promise, tragedy, courage, and rabid commitment to land, place, and lineage.

Being a pastor can be exhausting and draining. It's also a holy gift that allows an attentive ordained listener trusted access to a wonderful array of narratives and perspectives perhaps unmatched in any other job, weaving the hopes and dreams of a congregational assembly into weekly "news" that the preacher dares to call "good" in the eyes of a God who hopefully grants Sunday inspiration.

The South is also a region still recovering from a war that's "over" but not over in terms of the wounds that remain, often still festering and boiling into ugly exchange in our politics, hopes for the future, and opinions that form the direction of any community whose members are shaped by local history and family. I am a southerner—the good, the bad, the beauty, the all of it.

The gift of baptism, of course, defines my core identity, overriding all other genealogical and topographical inheritances. "When you were buried with him in baptism, you were also raised with him through faith in the power of God" (Col. 2:12). Christians have died and risen, grafted into the resurrection of Christ on this side of the grave (see Rom. 6:3–11). Your church's baptismal font is both tomb and womb. Family, region, race, and class all take a backseat, baptismally, to this surpassing sacramental identity.

But pastors like me may underestimate how jarringly countercultural such sacramental preaching really is in any region of the country with a history and set of assumptions similar to the South. My Lutheran church tradition includes certain safeguards for a minister who preaches prophetically, resulting at times in uncomfortable and even angry responses. Other clergy friends are not so lucky. Almost instant pastoral termination can result from a single unpopular sermon.

The previous chapter centered upon genealogy and inherited illness. In this chapter, I'll examine genealogy from the perspective of inherited incident, how *events* from long ago, occurring in a specific regional context, are also unavoidably an important part of us with the potential to shape future choices and vocational direction. These incidents from the past are certainly as removed from our control or manipulation as any illness we might inherit. But they still speak.

Like the previous chapter, I'll begin by describing an ancestor of mine. The following fictionalized short story is based upon real events and documented details from the past, inspired by an old photograph that currently resides in my South Carolina living room. I'll use the close-up details from the story to make wider observations about how God incorporates (literally, enfleshes) specific events from the genealogical past into any life.

SHERIFF FRANK OF CONCORD

My great-grandfather, for whom I'm named, looks at me with serious eyes, the sort of gaze that follows a person around the room and across more than a century of time. I stand by the refrigerator and then the kitchen window. The only way to escape his attention is to enter another room. I've considered moving him to a closet or an office file cabinet filled with other pairs of old and searching eyes, but there seems to be something he wants to tell me, so I leave him where he is, in the corner near the television, forming an interesting triangle of perspective whenever I watch something on the History Channel.

Frank was a tall man, six feet four inches, here wearing a double-breasted suit that hides a bit of paunch. Full cheeks, striped necktie, white shirt, pocket watch chain—the wardrobe of a serious lawman just starting work in an office of public trust. He's not wearing a gun, but I suspect it's holstered and loaded not far away, just outside the frame.

I like to think this was the suit he wore for a publicity photo when he became county sheriff at the tender age of thirty-six after an election that he barely won on the Republican ticket with just under nineteen hundred votes.

There is no smile in 1908; almost a frown, really. He looks tired. Few photographs from that era reveal much whimsy, but I suspect he had little to smile about in his new job as sheriff. The photo projects a confident countenance; a man not to be messed with.

One thing you cannot tell from his inescapable stare is that Sheriff Frank, in his first month in office, would preside over the last legal public hanging in the state of North Carolina. A black man named Will was accused of raping a white girl named Pearl, age sixteen. Close to two thousand people filled the Concord square a week before Christmas. My mother, an English teacher, now also gone, always said Will was a scapegoat for a lot of projected sugarcoated guilt among upstanding German immigrants.

"Rather ironic name for a town that hangs innocent citizens just before Christmas, don't you think, Reverend?"

She called me that (or "Rev") regularly after I graduated from seminary, about seventy-five years after Frank built the scaffold. Mom loved to use the word "ironic," but it's not the word that comes to mind as the sheriff's eyes follow his namesake around my living room.

*

Nobody else wanted to do it, and most men didn't know how. Agnes volunteered, for the record. Married fifteen years at the time to a man who had political aspirations even before dating commenced, this kind woman surely had no idea such dreams of service would involve wearing a badge.

Did she say, "I'll sew the condemned man's hood, Franklin; even criminals need a shroud to cover such darkness"?

As a daily reader of the Holy Scriptures, did Agnes thumb the pages of her well-worn Bible that December looking for assurance of the Lord's love, a Savior born to die who hung on a tree so long ago between two thieves? Did her three sons, ages five, seven, and nine, wonder what their mother was crafting with needle and thread those long nights upstairs even as the boys looked expectantly at the spruce beside the fireplace in the den, sawed, hauled, and decorated on Saint Lucia Day? Did she hear the nails pound Will's scaffold together those chilly afternoons, erected in the shadow of her house just a short walk from the jail?

Our family comes from a lengthy line of German Protestants. Ninety percent of the citizens of Cabarrus County were Lutherans, I once discovered, at the turn of the twentieth century. Ours is a faith centered upon grace, forgiveness, and divine time for repentance and change. Gifts of the Spirit offered for us all, regardless of merit. Brother Martin got that right during all his protests with the Roman Church hierarchy. Wonder why more Lutherans like me were not protesting as Will was led up the scaffold stairs, hooded?

I suppose it was inevitable (ordained?) that somebody in our family would become a pastor and attempt to speak up about all the fear and violence in the world. Pretty ironic (that favorite family word) that the angels first announced the good news with assurance and a booming "Fear not!" in a world so full of it.

The poor man was almost lynched just after Thanksgiving, even though young Pearl was unable to identify him in a lineup. Hundreds of men stormed the jail, yelling, throwing rocks, waving torches, daring the jailer to open the cell or they'd burn the building down. Will survived the night and was moved the next morning to Raleigh for safekeeping, then brought back to Concord for the hanging, the nativity of our Lord only a week away. Temporarily rescued for a later execution. I realize how strange that sounds.

Born to raise each child of earth. Born to give us second birth. Yes?

Will had no defenders. It's easy to look back over the years and consider what should have been done by any disciple of Christ.

Especially easy for me, I suppose, a repentant ghost who wishes he'd spoken up and who now gazes silently with regret and so much love upon my agonized great-grandson.

*

It's quiet on this fourth day of Christmas. I'm out for a walk, alone after dark, a bit dizzy from all the spiked eggnog but relieved that all the services are over, a lot of pastoral effort for a lot of people, many of whom I won't see again until next year at this time. Part of the call, I guess.

You don't have to walk very far in our little South Carolina town to receive an excellent star show, especially on a moonless night like this one. I stop and lean against an ancient oak on the far side of the middle school football field. A dog barks twice. All "the silent stars" go by, just like in the old hymn. I sit down and pray a while, looking up, eyes open.

I read the other day that scientists now believe that eight galaxies exist for every human being on the planet. And I'm staring into just this one—a Milky Way that seems to go on and on—honestly wondering if God really sees or even cares what we do in this vastness.

Is there generational improvement, moral headway, as time passes in a family? Is that part of what we mean in the creed each Sunday, in that line about believing in the communion of saints? That our ancestors are somehow rooting for us on the other side of death as they pass into the promised light where there is no night?

In my Christmas Eve sermon, I said something about the unlikely and marvelous nature of any birth. How, for example, if your great-grandparents hadn't gone on that blind date or their parents hadn't made that unexpected move to another state. And just think, I said, about dozens of other tiny details. Fiddle with just one of them and none of us would have been born. Jesus's birth is a rather preposterous miracle, I reminded my little flock, who've become used to me saying such things. But your next breath, the next beating of any heart, is also something completely and unpredictably marvelous and complex.

"Great sermon, Pastor Frank," many said at the door. "See you next Christmas, Rev," one of my favorite town skeptics offered with an irresistible laugh eliciting my own.

This fourth day of the season also happens to coincide with the church's remembrance of certain innocents, hundreds of children who died at the hands of a maniacal king who feared his power was slipping away to a new and improbable child-ruler whose birth was heralded by a certain star. So many innocents in this one starry galaxy.

Did anyone even try to speak up for the slaughtered children? Did anyone resist? Would I have resisted?

I close my eyes and rest against the old tree. His eyes were following me again earlier today. The sheriff of Concord still looks sad and tired. But I swear the longer I look at the photo, refusing to turn away from his story, it's like he's trying to tell me something.

*

The newspaper account in the *Evening Tribune* on December 18 that year reported that I shouted (with some volume) the following words before pulling the handle that released the trap at 11:16 a.m.—WILL BROWN, BEWARE THE DEATH!

Yes, all capitals. I did say something like that, I'll admit. But it wasn't shouted. I wasn't prone to shouting and can't ever recall using the word "beware." Agnes and I spoke quietly around the house, to each other and to the children. We were strict, yes, but not loud.

Beware. Be aware. Of death.

Not a bad idea, theologically, on this side of it. If I could tell my great-grandson anything now, it might be exactly that.

I see him tortured by our family history, wondering why I didn't act. Mostly my fault, I freely confess.

I still see Will's body fall through the false floor of the gallows, hear the horrible sound of his snapping neck, then the brief thrash of struggling feet finding no solid purchase, and the image of a father coming forward to receive his son's broken body.

The sight of his family gathered and weeping in the town square will never leave me. Will's ancestors—his own great-grandchildren—still reside in the county where I served and once wore the shiny badge of public trust. Only God knows the wide ripple effect from that awful day.

I was carrying out the law of the land. I was new at such, but that's the truth. And I was afraid. In a different way from so many gathered in the square that morning, hundreds of eyes upon their fledgling sheriff, but afraid all the same. Afraid of what people might think if I spoke up. Afraid of what might happen to my family. Afraid of what ugly forces might be released if I dared to differ.

Afraid? Absolutely. Of death? Probably.

But I so want to tell my great-grandson that fearfulness is no way for anyone to live. And that I'm so full of regret, even shame, even now, if that's possible for a specter like me.

I so much want to speak to him, to apologize for my cowardice, my complicity.

But I mostly want to tell him to trust the angels. Fear not, *fear not* the death. Be aware of it, yes, as a timekeeper, a gut-check, a reordering of priorities, a ticking invitation to change.

But there are worse things in life than dying for what you believe.

Living a lie, for instance.

There was never much concord in Concord. My silence helped no one. Truth is the only real freedom in a world where deception seems so much easier.

Be bold, I want to say. Speak up. Fear not. You're on the clock, pastor. Be aware of death and know there's so much more beyond it, past what humans can see, creating the potential for courage in any of us. I didn't quite believe it all back then.

*

My mother became obsessed with genealogy in the years before she died. I don't believe in ghosts. Resurrection, yes, at some point in the future. Ghosts? Come on.

But Mom swore she saw my great-grandfather once in the attic of her childhood home after he died. He was trying to tell her something. Maybe that explains her obsession with getting all the stories straight and passing on an accurate record of what happened in our family, as far back as she could find. She was tireless on her journeys into the past, twice visiting Salt Lake City to gain access to all the Mormons had gathered. They are intensely vigilant with ancestry, a desire to baptize their unwashed deceased in an odd ritual—celestial insurance, I suppose, for distant relatives who weren't already doused.

"The dead still speak, Reverend," she once told me with no hint of a smile.

I'm planning a trip to Concord next month. Haven't been there since I was a kid. The town has grown tremendously, a bedroom community these days for Charlotte and its millions, about thirty miles away.

There's something about that photo that won't leave me alone. The eyes are inescapable, as I've mentioned, but more. Is he cheering me on somehow? Is that one of the functions of the long dead?

I have a writer friend who says he always walks around the places he intends to depict in his novels, even continents away. Maybe I'll find Sheriff Frank and Agnes's old house—behind Saint James Lutheran, according to Mom.

And maybe I'll find the exact spot, if that's possible, where the gallows once stood and kneel in prayer for a good long while.

Pray that I might be given a voice to speak up, even now, when it's so much easier to stay silent.

*

I'm not sure what to believe about ghosts, how they may interact with us or why. Or if ghosts even exist. There's that weird scene with the Witch of Endor in First Samuel where a disguised and rather paranoid King Saul employs a reluctant medium to conjure the spirit of Samuel, resting and dead, who's not all that happy about his afterlife interruption (28:3–25). In one depiction of Jesus's nocturnal and buoyant amble toward their swamped sailing vessel, the disciples feel sure, initially, that they're witnessing the eerie approach of a ghost (Mark 6:47–52). Later, in a resurrection appearance, Jesus takes special pains to prove that he isn't a talking Casper the Friendly—after the disciples thought they were seeing a ghost—by flashing his wounds and munching on some grilled sea bass and hush puppies (Luke 24:36–43). And though I love the church's confessed belief, in the Apostles' Creed, of "communion" with saints who've preceded us, I have no explanation of how that really works, only that for me, it does.

I've never had any real and describable spiritual interaction with my great-grandfather, Sheriff Frank. But his life, what little I know about it, does seem to follow me around in a rather haunting (not ghostly) sort of way. I cannot accurately imagine what he must have thought as a regular churchgoing Lutheran who may have struggled with presiding over such brutality with internal misgivings, even though he was doing his job. But it's important for me to *try* and imagine his thoughts and actions leading up to and following the execution of Will Brown. This may have been the last public (and legal) hanging in the state of North Carolina, but it was certainly not the last brutal lynching in the state (or the South) by an angry gaggle of men and their gawking onlookers who regularly thought whatever warped sense of justice that may have ordered their days was just too damn slow.

I look at Sheriff Frank's picture a lot these days. At one time in my life, I was so embarrassed by the story that his photo resided in the bowels of a file cabinet in the back of a closet. Now he's out and viewable, partly because I want to believe that he struggled with his actions (and inaction), and partly because this incident partly shapes the person and pastor I've become through daily encounters with the teachings of Christ.

Slow to anger, God is described as merciful and gracious,

> "keeping steadfast love for the thousandth generation . . .
> but visiting the iniquity of the parents
> upon the children
> and the children's children,
> to the third and fourth generation." (Exod. 34:6–7)

These verses have bothered me a lot down through the years, wondering how children over a century removed from "the iniquity" can be held accountable for sins that occurred so long before their first breaths.

These days, I look at the verses differently. I'm not positive whether Will Brown was innocent, but I have a very strong suspicion that he was. And maybe I'm more sympathetic to the possible internal quandary of my great-grandfather than the real and accurate details might reveal.

But this event from over a century ago has formed me, much like other jarring events from your own genealogy have formed you. "The past is never dead," wrote William Faulkner in *Requiem for a Nun*. "It's not even past."

*

One of the parishes I served during my pastoral career is located in Abingdon, Virginia. Our three children grew up there, a beautiful setting in the mountainous southwest corner of the state, not far from the Appalachian Trail and serving as the western terminus of the Virginia Creeper Trail, one of the most famous cycling paths in the South, linking the town with the state's highest peaks. Two of my passions—cycling and backpacking—found regular expression from our Abingdon backdoor. After fourteen years, we departed for another call in South Carolina with many sad good-byes tearfully offered to a set of lifelong friends who assemble and still serve as Saint John Lutheran Church.

There was a great group of guys in Abingdon known as the Epiphany Players whose skits and annual spoofs on the news of the day were offered with great parish expectation in the annual talent show and youth fund-raiser celebrated just before Lent commenced, a sort of "Feast of Fools" historically associated with Mardi Gras.

One year, we devised a skit titled "Right Behind"—a spoof on the apocalyptic best seller *Left Behind*—which featured a men's support group who all suffered from the same affliction: a swollen starboard buttock, accentuated in the skit with a helium balloon. After watching a video (also produced by the Epiphany Players) featuring two Old Testament professors expounding upon the story of Balaam and his famous talking ass (Num. 22:22–40), the support group experienced healing when the balloons were "raptured" at skit's end. You may have to think about all this a while to get the puns flying around in "Right Behind." I can hear you groaning.

The year we left Abingdon, a couple months before my last Sunday in the pulpit, two guys in the acting troupe, John and Ed, secretly made a short film titled *Being Frank Honeycutt*. It was modeled upon the zany Charlie Kaufman movie *Being John Malkovich* (1999), where people stumble upon a dark portal that leads them into the brain and mind of the famous actor. Those who enter the portal see and experience what Malkovich might encounter on a given day, literally through his eyes, to great comedic effect.

I still don't know how John and Ed made the short (twenty-minute) film, but they somehow constructed an actual portal in their basement studio—a dark tunnel made of who knows what—that they both riskily entered with headlamps into my brain. Attendees at our good-bye dinner were invited into events and experiences (both real and fictionalized) that made their pastor tick, field reports from those who'd entered the portal and survived to tell the tale. Lots of laughter and tears, all around. I later learned that my own family members were willing accomplices in the video production. I still occasionally watch the film (a DVD gift from John and Ed). And I still laugh, cringe, and wince. They honored and also nailed me.

I mention these memories because the Bible—as anyone tries to make sense of their lives with the theological tools at our disposal—consistently offers a portal into the complicated minds of various characters who experience rather bizarre events that shaped them as flawed human beings whose lives are completely incomprehensible apart from those bizarre events. But still, they are somehow guided by a hidden God throughout the travail. It is highly unlikely that a particular Bible character (or a particular pastor, or a particular reader of this book) would emerge on the other side of the odd event unchanged. We look back on positive events and wonder what we'd be like if they hadn't occurred. But what about uncomfortable events? What if they had not occurred?

I'm thinking especially here of Joseph from the book of Genesis and the specific event where his siblings sell their young brother, the rather haughty dreamer, into slavery. The Bible offers an unusually detailed saga of the aftermath, inviting the reader into a portal of the protagonist's brain that could easily be called *Being Joseph of Egypt*.

*

Some advice: if you occasionally feel a little down about the state of your family, pick up the book of Genesis, especially chapters 37–50, and find odd comfort.[1] There's always that peculiar gift of dark perspective in reflecting upon one's relative pathology compared to someone else's problems. *At least I'm not as screwed up as these people.* Read Genesis; you'll feel better.

When Joseph was a teenager, his brothers loathed him. I admit to long-ago feelings of hostility toward my siblings, dreaming of their demise. It was worse in Joseph's family. The father of these twelve boys, Jacob, who had his own dark history of family dysfunction, was partial to Joseph and stupidly gave his favorite son presents (even when it wasn't his birthday) that the other brothers never received. Not hard to guess how that went over. One of these special gifts was a coat that may (or may not) have been of many colors (Gen. 37:3). It was certainly a fancy robe, and one of the many nails in the coffin of the brothers' growing resentment.

On top of all this, Joseph not only experienced a vivid dream life, he also shared his dreams with his family. One dream suggested that all of his brothers (and father!) would one day bow down and serve him. It's not the kind of thing you share around the breakfast table with your siblings who already despise you, but Joseph did.

The brothers become insanely angry and sell Joseph into slavery. They all collaborate in a lie and tell Daddy that wild bobcats attacked their brother in the wilderness. "Here's his bloody robe," they say with sad and straight faces. Feeling better about your own family history as you delve into these salacious details?

Joseph is presumed dead. But his adventures are really just beginning. Far from home, Joseph lands in prison after he resists the amorous advances of a lonely and desperate housewife, eventually rises to power through his precocious gifts of dream interpretation, and finally saves the day for Egypt by wisely managing a government grain-distribution operation during a time of drought.

At this point in the story, Joseph is the man. He is the go-to guy. When his brothers finally arrive in Egypt with empty stomachs, on the brink of starvation, and finally realize who Joseph really is, they cower before him like they're in the presence of the great and powerful Oz. They are, in short, toast.

"What if Joseph still bears a grudge against us and pays us back in full for all the wrong that we did to him?" (Gen. 50:15). Their fear is not unfounded.

When a state executes a criminal for a heinous crime, the real motivation for the execution is not deterrence of future crimes or to make society somehow safer. I'm opposed to capital punishment in all instances, but I would truly have more respect for those who mete out this punishment if they were honest and said, "This person whose life we're taking tonight deserves to die for the crime they committed. That's it, that's all."

We live in a payback world. I cannot recall how many divorce proceedings I've witnessed as a pastor where the real issue in a settlement was not really fairness. The real, unspoken, under-the-table issue was how to stick it to the guilty party in the marriage. To make them squirm and suffer for what they did. Revenge is among the most base and primitive of all human emotions. "I am your retribution," Donald Trump once claimed.

Knowing this, these cornered brothers hatch a lie. They lie to Joseph about their father's deathbed instructions concerning forgiveness. "Your father gave this instruction before he died, 'Say to Joseph: I beg you, forgive the crime of your brothers and the wrong they did in harming you'" (Gen. 50:16–17).

Forgiveness will be offered by Joseph. But there is not a shred of biblical evidence that Jacob ever said anything of the sort as he was dying. The brothers fall at Joseph's feet and beg for mercy. "We are here as your slaves" (50:18). Note the irony at this point: the dream Joseph had as a teenager has now come true.

It is here that the story, only a few verses from the end of the book of Genesis, takes a very unusual turn. "But Joseph said to them, 'Do not be afraid! Am I in the place of God? Even though you intended to do harm[2] to me, God intended it for good, in order to preserve a numerous people, as he is doing today. So have no fear; I myself will provide for you and your little ones.' In this way he reassured them, speaking kindly to them" (Gen. 50:19–21).

This story of radical forgiveness extended to wayward brothers is impressive enough. But for the purposes of this book, it can demote a surpassing curiosity: this circuitous saga (with its many twists and dark turns) was seemingly part of God's plan that led to a divinely imagined good, an outcome that had been swimming around in the Creator's mind for quite some time. Any changed small detail of this divine plan would severely alter the eventual outcome.

*

My wife, Cindy, and I rise early each morning to sing a hymn together without musical accompaniment, usually well before dawn. The hymn matches the tone and theology of the particular church-year season. Prior to the hymn, we also read aloud and discuss three texts from the daily lectionary—an Old Testament lesson, New Testament epistle selection, and a reading from one of the four Gospels, all arranged in a handy two-year index found in *Lutheran Book of Worship*—along with one psalm per morning, straight through the 150-prayer corpus. We then begin again with Psalm 1. The Bible texts move in sequence through a particular book before shifting to another.

The daily lectionary is a great gift in methodically guiding disciples through almost the entire Bible over percolated time. These early morning marital devotions are much easier to schedule, admittedly, since the kids are now grown and no school bus needs to be met. I've used the daily lectionary for decades in my personal devotions; together in our marriage only since Cindy's stroke.

Cindy suffered a stroke in April of 2021 that temporarily left her without a voice or use of her right arm. She's now resumed almost all previous activities through the gifts of excellent therapists. Speech sometimes remains a challenge. I wrote an article about the stroke and our decision to start reading the Bible texts aloud each morning:

> A retired high school teacher of English and public speaking, Cindy loves the cadence of words, the multiple meanings dis-

> covered in choice of inflection, the polyvalent possibilities lurking in tone and tenor. With her voice changed by the stroke, she wanted to hear the Bible spoken aloud by her husband. . . . We've imagined how young Samuel must have sounded in that classic encounter with Eli. How David's grief over the death of Absalom filled both heart and hallway. How the centurion at the foot of the cross offered his famous confession. How Esther found her brave tongue following Uncle Mordecai's encouragement. How the psalmist must have sounded while gazing at a night sky or imploring God's action in the face of injustice. How Paul crafted the right words to comfort ship passengers facing a wreck at sea. How Rhoda joyfully reported Peter's jailbreak to his disbelieving friends. And much more.[3]

The sun usually rises through the trees across the road just as we sing the last notes of the hymn and offer the Lord's Prayer. I then often consult Wikipedia on my cell phone and learn a bit about the life of the hymn writer. The results of this simple and quick search have been fascinating.

Martin Rinkhart, for example, is author of the hymn cited at the opening of this chapter, "Now Thank We All Our God," three verses whose historical context I never gave much thought to, perhaps preoccupied with a Thanksgiving feast with family that often followed the singing. Rinkhart died in 1649 after serving as a pastor in Germany through devastating famine, war, and a plague. At the height of these miseries, Rinkhart held funeral services for forty to fifty people *per day*. Many pastors fled their congregational calls, but not Rinkhart. This hymn was originally meant as a table prayer. Its tone, in private or corporate worship—especially given the suffering all around—is remarkable, striking a consistent stance of thanksgiving. "Keep us all in grace," writes Rinkhart, "and guide us when perplexed, and free us from all harm in this world and the next." *And in the next?*

That Pastor Martin's consistency in serving with praise was tinged with perplexity (and an honest wondering if this suffering might even hound his people beyond the grave) gives me a sort of angular hope and faith to keep pushing on through life's instances of meaninglessness. I once had two funerals in one week, but *Kyrie Eleison*, I experienced nothing like the suffering that washed over this hymn writer who, on a daily basis, bravely gave thanks even in the darkness of it all.

An American lawyer and Presbyterian church elder, Horatio Spafford (1828–1888), would later pen a beloved hymn, "When Peace like a River," popularly sung across many denominations and states in a still-new nation. Less well known is that Spafford wrote the hymn just after his four young daughters (with 222 others) died at sea on a transatlantic voyage when their steamship, on the way to England, was struck by another ship. His wife survived the tragedy. Spafford wrote the hymn as he traveled to meet her, inspired as he passed near the place on the ocean where the tragedy occurred. Spafford acknowledges his grief with the words: "when sorrows like sea billows roll."

What's less understandable, and utterly remarkable given the circumstances, is the faithful father's next line: "whatever my lot, thou hast taught me to say, it is well, it is well with my soul." Who has taught? And what exactly has been learned?

The hymns we sing—their content and often their context—slowly shape in gathered singers a faith that resembles Joseph's, the recipient of God's remarkable Egyptian providence, the divine "seeing ahead" revealed in that word's roots that twists and winds around tragedy, tempest, and, yes, genealogical time. Sad and specific events that no one would choose but that we all inherit, utterly agonizing details of the past without which any life would be remarkably different. What do these events mean for any of us who sometimes can barely squeak out muffled words of hymns that often elicit tears and wrenching memories?

English poet John Donne (1572–1631) wrote these odd words in "Meditation 17" of his *Devotions upon Emergent Occasions*: "No man hath affliction enough that is not matured and ripened by it, and made fit for God by that affliction."

Weird occasions (emergent or otherwise) litter anyone's past. Was Donne crazy? I cannot imagine offering his words in any hospital emergency room to which I've been summoned as a pastor. But I also shake my head in amazed admiration at people like Martin Rinkhart, Horatio Spafford, Joseph of Genesis standing before his guilty brothers, and so many others whose lives of faith are shaped by a tragic event. I want them to rail at God or at least curse their fate. Instead: an enviable testimony whose power and eventual meaning outlast the tragedy itself. The intended sibling "harm" (again, rendered "evil" in the Hebrew) cited by Joseph in Genesis 50:20 is recast, theologically, as part of a circuitous and rather baffling divine plan.

I've tried (and failed) to unearth more details concerning Sheriff Frank's motivations and possible misgivings concerning his role in the public hanging of a man who was most likely innocent of the crime for which he was executed. Like my great-aunt Eulie, my great-grandfather will most likely remain a figure from the shadows of the past, certainly an ancestor in my genealogical line who somewhat haunts me, but also definitely shapes decisions I've made, perhaps unconsciously.

Is it possible for any of us to look back on distant events from the past, part of our genetic inheritance, and say, with Joseph of Egypt, that God was somehow working through these horrible events to eventually bring about a positive outcome? Does the delayed grace and largesse of God simply take a while to work out, making its way through darkness to possible light? What does this roundabout path say about grace, about God? For the balance of this chapter, I'll focus on three words that attempt to answer these ponderous questions.

1. *Details*

Imagine for a moment that Joseph was not sold by the Ishmaelites[4] to a powerful Egyptian, Potiphar, and became a trusted servant in that house (Gen. 39:1–2). Imagine that Joseph did indeed succumb to the amorous advances of Potiphar's wife (Gen. 39:1–23). The story, with repeated sexual invitations from a powerful woman, is salacious enough. But let's say Joseph gives in to the temptation, an old story. Extramarital affairs litter the plodding path of many genealogies, fodder for multiple films and TV miniseries. Perhaps your own ancestral line features such mistakes.

Joseph is "handsome and good-looking" (39:6) and tries to go about his business. But "day after day" (39:10), he's sexually harassed by someone for whom consequences were probably rare. Had he not resisted, instead giving in to these advances, how would the wider narrative change? I suspect that Joseph would never have landed in prison (39:20), never found favor with the chief jailer (39:22), never needed occasion to display his prodigious gifts of dream interpretation (40:6–8), never found favor or met with Pharaoh after interpreting the powerful man's bizarre nocturnal visions (41:37–43), never saved many lives due to (mostly) wise grain management during a famine (41:53–57), and never seen his brothers again with certainly no dramatic and famous reconciliation between the twelve at the end of the book.

Joseph is indeed a flawed person. He is rather vain at times in the narrative. He cruelly toys with his brothers (and his father) before they discover his true identity. And, under the pretense of economic shrewdness, he enslaves impoverished victims of a famine who relinquish land in exchange for food (47:13–21), foreshadowing the future bondage of his own people under Egyptian rule in the book of Exodus. Perhaps Martin Luther had Joseph in mind while developing the famous phrase *simul justus et peccator*, "at the same time saint and sinner," the reformer's theological designation for any baptized person.

The narrative takes special pains to note that God repeatedly blesses Joseph's odd and bumpy journey to power: "the LORD was with him; and whatever he did, the LORD made it prosper" (39:23). *Whatever he did.* Would God have blessed and guided dissimilar "whatevers"? Possibly. But again, had Joseph chosen a different path in response to the seduction in the house of Potiphar, I suspect one of our favorite tales from the book of Genesis would be vastly different.

The details matter in our lives and to God. Again, fiddle slightly with only one or two details from your genealogical past, and an entire ball of twine involving destiny and perhaps chance, waiting to become your future, quickly unravels.

In her poem "If We Are All Unremarkable Angels,"[5] Anna Elkins describes an encounter she once had with a young child, a toddler, who came running toward her one morning on the edge of a lake in New Zealand, lined with colorful pebbles. Just before reaching her, the child stops, stoops down to select a stone, and presents it to her, a stranger, as a gift. Empty-handed, on the run, the little boy "found what he needed just when he needed it." She thanks the child, puts the stone in her pocket, and watches his joyful return to a family who are all beaming in the near distance, each shining with beauty. The poet wonders whether this family may be angels and whether we "take turns playing angel," leading the lost back up a path, offering timely gifts like that colorful stone, "a talisman of praise."

This poem reminds me of Joseph's life—any life, really, open to a God who works through seemingly innocuous details that might seem small in the moment but can forever change a life as we notice them, their steady beckoning and guidance like illumined bits of bread along a broken path, divine gifts leading us to new insights and new directions, just when we needed them.

2. *Decisions*

If we miss the details, don't notice the guidance or divine prodding, or simply stubbornly refuse even the clear directional invitation, what then?

I recall a warm evening in 1988. Our first child, then two, was asleep in a back bedroom of our church parsonage in the Shenandoah Valley. Cindy and I sat at the kitchen table, sipping tea and looking at each other the way young couples facing an important decision tend to look at one another. The windows were open, no air-conditioning in the house at the time. A fan hummed. The strange ground emergence of seventeen-year locusts occurred that year, still pretty raucous even after sunset—mating, calling, and dying in a quick burst of passion, oddly setting the seventeen-year clock again in motion. There was a one-way lane behind our house that led to a narrow viewing place where Hannah, our daughter, and her dad, the pastor, could go for a short walk and watch the cows, her favorite a white-and-black Holstein we dubbed "Circle Around the Eye" with an accompanying tiny finger-motion circling her own eye. Good memories, figuring out how to be a pastor, how to be young parents, how to be faithfully and happily married—instructions not available for any of these roles in a handy one-size-fits-all format.

Even while seriously dating at a summer camp where we met, we'd talked about our commitment to adoption. Cindy got pregnant during the fourth year of our marriage, my last at seminary. Now settled into our first call in Virginia, we looked at each other across that table that night. I can't remember which one of us asked: "Are we really going to do this?"

We learned of a little girl in El Salvador, five months old. Her birth mother, caringly we're convinced, left her baby in a public hospital two days after the birth. A local orphanage (destroyed in an earthquake not many years later), short-staffed with a small team of courageous nuns, received the baby into their care among twenty crib-mates. The nuns were so busy that bottled formula was often propped against a crib slat. The babies learned how to eat without being held.

We didn't have much money. I approached a generous local banker, Bob, a parishioner, who without hesitation helped with Cindy's plane ticket. Gobs of paperwork, translated from English to Spanish. Immigration documents misplaced (a kind word for "lost") by an overworked government official in Washington, DC.

A kind social worker and her equally kind husband, an attorney, in San Salvador, the capital city. A solo, three-day trip by Cindy, into a country ravaged by war, just days before Christmas after months of planning, prayer, and worry. A happy entourage waiting at Dulles airport with flowers and balloons. A big sister feeding her new sister her first bottle on American soil. "Give Marta some milk," Hannah instructed. We all laughed, and cried. Today Hannah is an attorney who fights for access to justice and lifts up the poor. She reminds me of her biblical namesake who sang of a God who "raises up the poor [and] lifts the needy" (1 Sam. 2:8).

We kept the name the nuns gave our new baby, Spanish for "Martha." Now, almost forty years later, with Marta serving as a lead preschool teacher in inner-city Columbia, South Carolina, it strikes me how she, like her sister, also embodies the persistent personality of her sassy biblical namesake—a woman who would not keep quiet about life's sadness nor its extravagant possibilities (John 11:21–22).

Three years later, we adopted another child, a beautiful biracial boy named Lukas who came to us at four days old through a very faithful attorney who specialized in placing at-risk children. Unmarried and single in a small Tennessee town, with a father who frowned on racial mixing, Lukas's birth mother also made a courageous and painful decision. And these days I also wonder if Lukas's name emerged for a reason more than our simple love of the sound of it. A soft-hearted kid who brought home hamsters from school and doted upon a series of spoiled cats and a dog, he's now studying social work in a master's program, an echo of a Bible character named Luke, a physician and local healer (Col. 4:14).

All of us—the flawed parents and our three children—have had challenges. What family doesn't? Interracial families built by adoption have been questioned by social workers in recent years who wonder if adoption possibly erases sympathies to and celebration of racial identity.[6] It's a valid and important question. Our motivation, principally, was born out of love. Children needed a home and our hearts were open. In retrospect, Cindy and I would do nothing differently.

It started with a decision, across from each other, sipping tea among the cicadas, creatures hatched over percolated time. A decision that forever shaped and formed the direction of a young family and its five members. A decision (I cannot help but wonder) that may have been subconsciously born at the scene of an old gallows in 1908 in Concord, North Carolina. That night in the Shenandoah Valley, Sheriff Frank's name never came up. I honestly did not even know his story then.

But if the God of Psalm 139 is indeed aware of "all the days that were formed for me, / when none of them yet existed" (139:16), then I must conclude that the decision we made at that table that night, over tea, was more than accidental, and not even remotely by chance. Looking ahead, how will these decisions matter one hundred years from now?

3. *Dying*

Details and decisions drive and shape the direction of any life, any household. It's only natural to pose a series of ifs: If I didn't meet her then, or go there? If I hadn't taken this course, or gone to that school? If we'd slept late that morning, not chosen that particular trail in the woods, or turned down that crazy but compelling job offer instead of accepting it? Hundreds of different lives, reasonable outcomes for the same person, hinge upon details and decisions that in turn affect genealogical sleuthing and eventual insight. These observations may sound obvious; they are also mind-boggling. Is there a guiding principle in Christian theology to hang our baptismal hats upon?

I've long been intrigued by the details and decisions peppering Acts 16:6–15. This lesson, liturgically, is assigned during the Easter season (Cycle C) and occurs in Acts 16 just after Paul and Silas meet Timothy (child of an interethnic marriage), whose positive local reputation among the Lystra believers sparks wider missionary travels for the trio (16:1–5), and just before Paul and Silas are tossed into prison for disrupting the local economy, which then sparks a rather fantastic jailbreak (16:16–40). The entire chapter is one of my favorites in Acts. I can see why lectionary drafters placed this remarkable narrative of death, birth, new life, and new directions during the fifty days of Easter.

For purposes connected to the three leading words in this section ("details," "decisions," and now "dying"), indulge me in offering a small chunk of one of my past sermons that ponders the circuitous and quite odd nature of the geographical path of Paul and Silas after they meet up with Timothy and embark upon travels filled with as many twists and turns as any Agatha Christie novel. A map of the region may be helpful as we sift through geography locales. This is how the sermon began. I spoke these words rather breathlessly, as the text seems to suggest:

> Check closely to see if I get the details from this story fairly straight. On a missionary journey, Paul and his companions are forbidden by the Holy Spirit to speak the word in Asia. Even though churches will eventually appear in Asia, there's a big divine stop sign at the regional line so they bop over towards Bithynia and try to share the gospel there, but nothing doing. "Keep on heading west," says the Spirit who seems to be providing their road map.
>
> Averted in Asia and barred from Bithynia, Paul tacks over to Troas (named for ancient Troy). Troas is on the edge of the Aegean Sea, a coastal town. Paul has never been further away from home in his life. Maybe they breathe some ocean air. Maybe they grab some seafood at a local diner or check-in to some bargain beach motel. Maybe they begin to wonder a bit about all these unusual directional signposts from the Holy Spirit. Here at the edge of their known world, there's a pause in the journey.

So Paul beds down for the night, water lapping in his dreams; more bits of bread dropped along his missionary path. A man from Macedonia speaks in a night vision. "Get over here please and help us." (I've no idea how Paul recognizes this man *as* a Macedonian; he's never been to Macedonia in his life. Maybe the guy is wearing a university t-shirt.)

Paul awakens and boards a boat—sea breeze in his hair; lots of time to think. The first day they travel about 80 miles over to Samothrace, an island eight miles long with tall mountains. Tempting to stick around and explore, but they were back on the boat the next day: 70 nautical miles to Neapolis (literally "Newtown"), aptly named, for all this is brand-spanking new for Paul.

But there's more. They disembark the boat in Neapolis and hike about ten miles inland to Philippi. (A curious little cuss, I also looked up this distance.) They look around the city a few days. On the Sabbath, Paul and Company are led to a river and a particular spot that looks like a place of prayer. A woman shows up; a fairly wealthy woman, a cloth merchant with a penchant for purple. Her name is Lydia. She likes what she hears and her entire household is dunked into the mercy and grace of God.

This river encounter—born from a series of stop signs, sea crossings, and dreams in the night—is how the church in Philippi came to be. It's why we have the Book of Philippians in the New Testament, the very first Christian congregation in Europe. For some sitting here this morning, this church fans out over the centuries into your genealogy (perhaps) and mine.[7]

What are careful readers of Scripture to make of these curious details and decisions? First, and perhaps primarily, I would love for the Holy Spirit to place a divine stop sign in front of some of my actions and keep me from doing boneheaded things that, in retrospect, are regrettable and entirely preventable. Perhaps a few desired stop signs are also coming into your own mind as you read this book.

Second, I realize that when we hear folk talk this way—arranging their lives by listening to dreams, night voices, or spiritual gusts of wind—it often all seems rather hokey and contrived. I'm convinced that God sometimes speaks to us in dreams because our waking-day defenses are otherwise erected, suspicious, and always on guard. I'm also pretty certain that we should choose wisely concerning the next-morning audience of these dreams, lest hearers begin to question our sanity.

Third, there's a delicate balance here between human freedom and any revealed divine intervention that seems to remove choice (more on this in the next chapter). God said "go" to Moses. The poor guy didn't want to go and offered a variety of valid excuses (Exod. 4:1–17), a relatable tension in many lives of faith. There's an amusing contradiction between two of the most popular slogans that consistently escape from my (and perhaps your) mouth. The sayings are these: (a) "It's a free country," and (b) "There ought to be a law against that." There is probably an irreconcilable tension between destiny, God's justice, and human freedom.

Fourth, Lydia, so instrumental in forming the church in Philippi, is mentioned only here and one other time in the New Testament (in the same chapter) as she provides sanctuary for the two jailbreakers (Acts 16:40). But her importance in helping start this fledgling congregation must have been immense. Small details involving obedience to the Spirit's nudges sometimes result in a very large future impact.

All of this suggests a trio of travelers (Paul, Silas, and Timothy) so in tune with the Spirit's guidance, "thy will" being done, that sacramental images of dying and rising come to mind—dying to their own traveling desires, dying to their own opinions concerning mission route, dying to their own arguments of intellectual resistance, and principally dying to self. Taken together, these are the spiritual characteristics of a disciple. "If any want to become my followers, let them deny themselves and take up their cross daily and follow me" (Luke 9:23). This may seem like controlled robot-hood. I prefer to call it the language of baptism.

I find it provocative that our traveling trio was led to a river (Acts 16:13) in Philippi after their improbable journey by sea to get there.

Everyone born into the church via the gift of baptism was once right there at Troas, so to speak, with Saint Paul at the edge of the sea, on the banks of a river. Farther away from home than we've ever been, received into a new family and a new home. With the coaxing and call of God, we dove in, listening for what's next.

*

This chapter has explored the role of inherited incident in the unfolding of any disciple's life, in my own case a scarring past hanging. I suspect we'd be very different people without these events, but at whose expense does a possible future outcome occur?

The story of Saint Paul's surprising sea and land journey, guided by a spiritual compass, suggests a sacramental response, more fully developed in chapter 6. For now, however, I want to linger with the vexing genealogical questions of destiny and free will.

Chapter 5

DESTINY, CHANCE, AND FREE WILL

"We come with self-inflicted pains of broken trust
and chosen wrong,
half-free, half-bound by inner chains, by social
forces swept along,
by pow'rs and systems close confined, yet seeking
hope for humankind."

—Brian Wren, "Great God, Your Love Has Called Us" (verse 2)

"He destined us for adoption as his children through Jesus Christ, according to the good pleasure of his will, to the praise of his glorious grace that he freely bestowed on us in the Beloved."

—Ephesians 1:5–6

In college, I spent five summers working at two different camps in the mountains of western North Carolina and foothills of upstate South Carolina—low pay, long hours, great lifelong friends, and invaluable experience working with children, youth, and adults with special needs, encounters that would greatly shape my future vocation as a pastor.

My cabin of fourth-grade boys one of those five Julys was a group of eight rambunctious Lutheran kids hailing from all over the

Southeast. They were fun and exhausting. We laughed and played hard with all the activities of camp life—swimming, hiking, crafts, mud fights when it rained, raucous dining hall songs, active Bible study, evening vespers, and much more. A rather laughable hour each afternoon following lunch was called F.O.B., Flat on Bunk, a nap for the guys that, of course, did not occur. They (and I) did sleep quite well at night, exhausted from the stimulation of the day.

One night around 2:00 a.m., I got up to use our cabin bathroom; all the boys were asleep. While I was sitting there on the pot in a sleepy stupor, an alarm clock went off somewhere in the bathroom. After mouthing a whispered "what the hell?" expression, I rose to locate the source of the noise, lifted the ceramic lid, and, incredulous, found the ringing alarm clock secured in the tank of the commode above the water. Camp alarm clocks were all wind-ups back then. I managed to turn the darn thing off before it woke any of the campers, went back to bed, and started to plot payback for a couple of witty friends who, I was pretty sure, were the source of the prank.

At 2:30 a.m., another clock went off, retrieved from a cabin rafter. The kids slept on. I stood in the middle of the cabin, no longer chuckling, and listened. The cabin was filled with audible ticking. With a flashlight, I searched and found four more clocks, set to go off at various time intervals.

Pleased with myself, at breakfast the same morning I bragged to three clock-planting suspects, each feigning innocence, that I'd found all their cute time bombs.

The entire camp was called into the dining hall, noisily taking seats. Just before 8:00 a.m., in the mass silence observed before the breakfast prayer, another alarm clock went off. It didn't take long to discover the thing had been duct-taped under my seat. I later learned that almost all three hundred diners except me were aware of what was going to happen at 8:00 a.m.

I was never able to concoct equitable revenge that summer for such a creative practical joke. I was, however, rather confused a week or so later when I started pulling out springs and metal parts from the bottom of a washer tub after doing a load of dirty clothes, thinking the washer was broken. After pulling out a clock face along with a pair of clean socks, I laughed out loud. Here was a clock I'd missed, hidden in the bottom of my laundry bag.

*

Human beings celebrate, agonize, laugh, cry, plan, grieve, work, and play during their cumulative days on the planet, along with countless other verbs describing the gift of any life. Like my father, and his dad before him, I now read the obituaries of our paper rather closely to keep track of the county personalities who've passed on, characters who've led interesting lives even though they've never been featured in the national news.

The Bible makes the audacious claim that "all the days that were formed" for each of us (even before we existed) were known by the Creator and recorded "in [God's] book" (Ps. 139:16). The psalmist follows this verse with an incredible understatement that I'm sure Mel Brooks could make a movie out of: "How weighty to me are your thoughts, O God!" (139:17).

What are thoughtful people of faith to make of these claims? Do we subscribe to an ebullient embrace of unquestioned providence?[1] Do we join a rather hopeless Job from the Old Testament—who's rather had it with the explanation of his life troubles from well-meaning friends—when he dejectedly asks, "Shall we [my hope and I] descend together into the dust?" (Job 17:16). Do we see life as a series of alarm clocks, planted by an all-knowing and all-seeing divine hand who maybe knows that we'll answer some of their urgent rings but will invariably miss a few? Is it more likely (to use Brian Wren's words that begin this chapter) that we are "half-free, half-bound by inner chains," an apt description of any life whether the chains are self-inflicted, inherited, or accidental? What is destiny, according to God, and how does this shape or handcuff my own free will and decision making?

CHAPTER 5

✶

Like hidden alarm clocks jolting you awake in the night, I suspect a series of old stories, roads taken and not taken, important choices could have shaped your life and those you love. We sometimes dream of another life that could have easily occurred for us, a life that still lingers in our imaginations and waking days. If God knows the shape of our days before we're even born, as the psalmist claims, are we powerless to become anything other than who we've become? Is "choice" even the right word to describe the origins of our respective vocations? Given the agonizing inheritance of a public hanging presided over by my great-grandfather, and the sad illness and its aftermath experienced by my great-aunt, was a clergy vocation often centered upon suffering and service always part of my own destiny?

My thinking on these questions finds a bit of clarity in a challenging hike I once took in Acadia National Park on the Maine coast with an old friend, Howard, on the very fun but rather nerve-racking Precipice Trail. The trail begins near sea level and rises one thousand feet in less than a mile, quite steep, over and under boulder fields, along skinny ledges with a series of iron handholds, up several ladders driven into rock face, arriving at the summit of Champlain Mountain, with breathtaking views of Frenchman Bay and Bar Harbor throughout the hike. I've done a lot of hiking (including the entire length of the 2,100-mile Appalachian Trail from Maine to Georgia) but have never encountered a trail that required so much concentration and pretty intense thought with almost every step. Park rangers strongly discourage making the hike in wet or foggy weather and recommend hiking in only one direction: *up*, with an easier side trail for the descent. The trail is also closed part of the year when peregrine falcons make their nests on the rocky ledges all along the trail. Even rest stops—to park your butt and regain your breath—require a bit of thinking. The trail is incredibly rewarding, offering outstanding views and a sense of accomplishment, but it's not for the faint of heart or anyone that's vertigo-inclined. Howard and I started laughing, maniacally, in spots as we considered our next steps.

This challenging hike reminds me of several of the questions I've been posing throughout this book. There are not an infinite number of ways to navigate the Precipice Trail, and the trail leads to a particular summit, not a variety of summit choices. But the actual steps one takes along the route (and missteps requiring a quick turnaround and rethinking of one's last choices) are indeed abundant and varied. Some missteps can lead to injury, I suppose. And not to be morbid, but some people have gone against counsel, hiked in the rain, lost balance on a slippery ledge, and fallen to their deaths on this trail. Bad results can occur in any life, sometimes through no one's fault (see the book of Job), but also as a result of foolish choices, the consequences of which are difficult to rewind.

The analogy is not perfect, but a Precipice Trail hike can be compared with the components of almost any life: (1) There are risks involved (and also rewards) for assuming the challenge; (2) no one is forcing you to start the hike and no one is controlling your every step, with options in the going even though the goal may be unchanging; (3) it's possible to backtrack, rethink the route a bit, and continue on.

Again, an imperfect analogy, but this one attempts to blend the ideas of divine guidance and human freedom without resorting to a conclusion that we're all destined automatons with no input in determining life's vocational route, a route filled with several challenging decisions, call them precipices. We indeed face choices, several of which we may regret taking (or not taking), but perhaps life's baptismal trajectory remains, generally, on a path of service and discipleship in answer to God's call.

To piggyback on this idea, I'd like to examine one day in the life of Jesus, a day filled with several choices and changes in direction that started and ended in a fashion that I very much doubt he had in mind at breakfast but remained in concert with God's will for his life. With an open Bible, dear reader, please take a look with me at Matthew 9:9-26.

*

I realize the story doesn't actually mention a particular day, but pretend it's a Tuesday as Jesus sits down for a meal (9:11) in a house. He's just called Matthew (the notorious IRS man) from his day job.

Matthew is *at work* when Jesus calls him, and the tax man gets up and follows. He's right in the middle of a typical "nine to five" when Jesus strolls into his life. And nowhere do I see any ecclesiastical caveats like: "Follow me when you have time to follow" or "Follow me on Sunday mornings" or "Follow me at your own convenience." No, *it's a workday* for Matthew, and Jesus calls the little tax cheat away from his livelihood and wants him to start living a new way right there and then. Please notice: moneymaking takes a back seat to following Jesus; "gainful employment" will now be reshaped and newly envisioned with the gospel clearly in mind. In short, God will not be kept in a convenient box called Sunday.

The Bible calls what follows "a dinner" in verse 10, but the time of day is actually ambiguous in the Greek, so let's call it lunch. A Tuesday lunch-gathering with Jesus. He's a bit worn out, I'd say, from all his travels, consorting and cavorting with tax collectors, prostitutes, welfare frauds, ex-cons, adulterers, and those with no green card. The man needs nourishment, right? He's human, say the creeds; got hungry and thirsty, weary from all this ministry of crossing tracks to include people others hated, segregated.

Just when Jesus says "pass the peas" at lunch that Tuesday, some church people and their pastors, members of a large local and prominent congregation, burst through the door in full outraged entourage and demand to know what in the world Jesus thinks he's doing. They actually corner his followers and lividly inquire whether Jesus has any sense of propriety at all. Does he have any idea who these people *are* with whom his bread is being buttered?

And right there (I've always loved this about Jesus) the man taps a water glass with a spoon and delivers a zinger of a sermon—quite short but devastatingly pointed—about mercy and love and healing and how the self-righteous so often miss out on grace (9:12–13). It was quite a homily, and I'd say it silenced the lunchroom interlopers, who exit huffily to now talk about this man in the parking lot. "Pass the biscuits, please," says Jesus, I'm imagining.

But just before the next bite, some disciples of John the Baptist barge in with a question about fasting. "God says we're supposed to sacrifice and look forlorn when thinking about divine things, and here you are stuffing your face all the time, Jesus. What's up with that?" (9:14, translation by FGH).

With no hint of annoyance that the mashed potatoes are getting cold, Jesus delivers a second little homily to a completely different audience (at that same Tuesday luncheon) and says something about new wine and old wineskins and how mixing the two will leave you with fermented grape juice exploding in your face. His questioners look at one another, a bit flummoxed by this vexing tale from the vineyard (9:15–17).

I absolutely love verse 18. "*While he was saying these things to them . . .*" That is, smack-dab in the middle of that second sermon to that second group of lunch interrupters, between mouthfuls and obviously unscheduled, a leader of the synagogue bursts in and kneels before Jesus. Try to imagine this. A grieving father interrupts those *other* interlopers who in turn had also intruded uninvited to interrupt a prior set of unexpected questioners. It's the same meal. Two sermons have been offered and now this. The side dishes, I suspect, are a bit tepid by now.

So this poor man, a father in a puddle of woe, throws himself on Jesus and says, "My daughter is dead, but I know she'll be okay if you just come. Please come" (9:18, trans. FGH). And so Jesus, God bless him, gets up right then and there with the napkin still under his chin and heads down the road with this grieving daddy, leaving the astonished lunchroom guests with mouths agape and more than a few leftovers.

I generally clear the calendar for funerals. There's something about a dead person that demands one's full and immediate attention. Jesus, surely, will make a beeline for this little girl's bedside and do his thing. But on the way from that lunch filled with various interruptions, a final interrupter on this one Tuesday in the life of Jesus pops out of the crowd and reaches out for the man.

"Maybe if I just touch him," she thinks. "I don't need much, just the fringe of his shirt" (9:21, trans. FGH). But Jesus gives her a lot more than that. He stops. He chats and heals. After all the other shifts and changes in this one day, enough interruptions for *a year* of Tuesdays, Jesus stops on his way to a funeral and tenderly encounters this needy woman who's been bleeding for twelve long years.

And I know what I would have probably said. Something like: "Woman, do you have any idea what kind of day I'm having here? Take a number, will you?" But remarkably, unbelievably, Jesus stops and kindly offers a touch and a word before proceeding on to the bedside of that little girl. If you've been counting, this is the fourth interruption in a scene that began with a simple bite of lunch.

After the healing of the little girl, preceded by a crowd who pointedly laughs at Jesus (9:24), please notice Matthew's summary of this section: "The report of this spread throughout that district" (9:26). The report of *what* exactly? And one quick answer, of course, is that the report is full of the news of that little girl running and jumping again. The miraculous is always something of a head-turner in the Bible.

But maybe "the report" on Jesus also included the various twists and turns and interruptions and calm clarity of the man when he seemed on the verge of being pecked to death by a gaggle of ducks. "Why this, Jesus?" "Why that?" "Why them?" "Please do this for me, Jesus."

And he handled it all with honesty, grace, and aplomb. If you're looking for miracles from this particular Tuesday, please don't overlook that one. Some wise person once said something like, "Churches sometimes spend far too much time thinking about how to plan for ministry, how to strategize for ministry. But ministry is not something you 'go and do' in neat little time blocks. It's something you do as you go."

It's the whole day that Matthew wants me to notice, with twists and turns and precipitous decisions far more challenging than that trail in Maine, forever changing the way I look at Tuesdays and all the days God gives any of us.

Are these more than simple "chance" encounters for Jesus, who, admittedly, was much more in tune with the prodding of the Holy Spirit than some plebian disciple like me? His "destiny" was the cross and resurrection anyway, right? Why not have a wildly, unexpected, gear-changing day when you're the Son of God with an impressive genealogy filled with misfits and their résumés featuring odd shifts in direction?

I want to make the case that Jesus's clear sense of identity—knowing "that he had come from God and was going to God" (John 13:3)—gave him freedom to decide and act in the moment, avoiding any sense of some robotic "predestination" controlling each day and movement, but also a certain freedom within a wider obedience to a vocation of denial of self and embracing a life on the road to Jerusalem that looked a lot like a cross even before he died.

"Follow me," Jesus says to the tax collector (Matt. 9:9) who, after doing so, apparently witnessed all the twists and turns of that one Tuesday. Those two small but life-changing words of discipleship lead us into the next chapter, life in the beloved community formed in baptism.

"I am learning from Jesus," wrote Dallas Willard (1935-2013), "to live *my* life as he would live my life if he were I. I am not necessarily learning to do everything he did, but I am learning how to do everything I do in the manner that he did all that he did."[2]

Read those two sentences again, slowly, keeping Jesus's multidirectional Tuesday in mind. How does baptism both interrupt and shape the living of days granted by a Creator who somehow saw all the ticks and tocks "that were formed for me, / when none of them as yet existed" (Ps. 139:16)?

Chapter 6

BAPTISM AND THE NEW FAMILY LINE

"A crowd was sitting around [Jesus]; and they said to him, 'Your mother and your brothers and sisters are outside, asking for you.' And he replied, 'Who are my mother and my brothers?' And looking at those who sat around him, he said, 'Here are my mother and my brothers! Whoever does the will of God is my brother and sister and mother.'"

—*Mark 3:32–35*

"So if you have been raised with Christ, seek the things that are above, where Christ is, seated at the right hand of God. Set your minds on things that are above, not on things that are on earth, for you have died, and your life is hidden with Christ in God."

—*Colossians 3:1–3*

Not long into the Gospel of Mark—after Jesus's baptism, after forty days in the wilderness with satanic temptations and wild beasts, after several healings and pronouncements that seem to tick people off and result in the repeated, pointed question, *Why* (2:7, 16, 18, 24), and after the call of his first disciples—word gets back to the family of Jesus, loved ones who are pretty convinced their family member has gone off the deep end. When his family hears of the crowds starting to follow Jesus, they schedule what's now known as an *intervention*: "they went out to restrain him, for people were saying, 'He has gone out of his mind'" (3:21).

That must have been a bit wounding for Jesus to learn of his mom and siblings "standing outside" (3:31), assembled and waiting to confront him about this odd behavior and take their boy back home to a nice room and perhaps a visit from the local doctor bearing appropriate pharmaceuticals. Mark doesn't indicate that Jesus was embarrassed by this attempted intervention, but I like to think there was at least a short pause in his teaching that day as he received the message of their presence from a courier and considered their intentions just outside. A short pause before he offered a zinger that surely raised Mary's eyebrows when it got back to her, reshaping the notion of Christian family subsequently formed by baptism and attention to the word of God.

Who are my mother and my brothers? "Not necessarily those standing outside, waiting to take me away," Jesus seems to say, "not really blood kin at all, but instead all of you here who are obedient to God's will. That's my real family."

I'm not sure any equivalent of Mother's Day existed in first-century Palestine. I do suspect it was rather tough being the mother of Jesus. Mary "pondered" (Luke 2:19) the words of the shepherds three decades prior in Bethlehem after their vivid report of an angelic visitation announcing news of her special baby. The word for "ponder" in the Greek is *symballo*. The stems in this word are *ballo* (to throw) and *sym* (together). As Mary ponders at the manger, she is throwing new ideas together in her mind and heart. Rattling around in her imagination, thrown together, are thoughts that perhaps began germinating after Gabriel's visit and the subsequent hike to Elizabeth's house (Luke 1). The pondering surely continued when she received word that her increasingly famous son just redefined the notion of what a family is and who his true relatives really are. It's important to imagine Mary walking away from Jesus's teaching venue that day, to imagine what she was pondering and what it all meant.

Her thoughts (and our own pondering) in reaction to these rather stark words about kinship connect to the genealogical ruminations we've been posing in this book. How does baptism interrupt and reshape our notions of where we've come from and God's guidance through even the most complicated of genetic inheritances?

✶

Several times in the New Testament, baptism is referred to as a death. There are certainly other biblical baptismal metaphors: new life; welcome into the church, the body of Christ; forgiveness of sin; bestowal of spiritual gifts. But the idea of dying with Christ in the saving waters confronts a reader of Scripture like a recurring drumbeat:

> Do you not know that all of us who have been baptized into Christ Jesus were baptized into his death? (Rom. 6:3)

> But if we have died with Christ, we believe that we will also live with him. (Rom. 6:8)

> I have been crucified with Christ; and it is no longer I who live, but it is Christ who lives in me. (Gal. 2:19b–20)

> I want to know Christ and the power of his resurrection and the sharing of his sufferings by becoming like him in his death. (Phil. 3:10)

> He has rescued us from the power of darkness and transferred us into the kingdom of his beloved Son. (Col. 1:13)

> When you were buried with him in baptism, you were also raised with him through faith in the power of God. (Col. 2:12)

> For you have died, and your life is hidden with Christ in God. (Col. 3:3)

> You have been born anew, not of perishable but of imperishable seed, through the living and enduring word of God. (1 Pet. 1:23)

How might a joyful embrace of this idea—dying with Christ in baptism—shape and reframe any reflection upon one's specific genealogical inheritance? Did Jesus have it bluntly right about the new family, sending his relatives, his genealogical kin, away that day? As a Christian, who really are my mother and siblings? Blood kin are certainly important, determining (and sometimes haunting) daily life. DNA saliva tests, all the current rage, can be both revealing and fascinating. Genetic revelations are empowering and may lead to peace of mind, health-wise. Baptismally speaking, however, is water even thicker than blood? To begin a response to this sacramental question, I need to tell you about a funeral I once helped with.

*

My best friends in seminary decided not to become pastors. I remain close to several clergy guys from the class of 1985 at Lutheran Theological Southern Seminary, but those I spent the most time with during those years in Columbia, South Carolina, took other vocational paths after graduation. Maybe I was drawn to them because there was part of me that was also hesitant about life as a pastor.

My friend Bill, a hiking companion throughout my first year in seminary—we hiked eight days (eighty miles) in the Nantahala Range of western North Carolina that February without seeing any other humans, nor the sun for the first seven days—decided to become a ranger in Shenandoah National Park; he was a naturalist who could identify (complete with genus name) practically anything growing, wildflowers especially. My wife, Cindy, and I were backpacking through the park in the summer of 1984, heading south on the Appalachian Trail. We knew we'd be meeting up with Bill at some point in the park but didn't know exactly where or when.

We came upon a tall, rectangular concrete post at the confluence of several trails, a metal band attached to the top of the post listing several mileage facts concerning various compass directions. Tucked into the metal band was a paper note with our names in a familiar script. "I'm at the spring about a quarter-mile from here, come on down."

We found Bill sitting beside the spring, poring over notes for a program he'd give that evening at Loft Mountain campground on June wildflowers in the park—Solomon's seal, spiderwort, lady's slipper (pink and yellow), jack-in-the-pulpit, wild columbine, and many more. He was preparing to enter a pulpit different from mine but one still brimming with the grandeur and complexity of God.

A little more than a decade after this meeting beside a spring, Bill's diagnosis of brain cancer rocked my life, my pastoral work, my trust in God. I'd break into tears at traffic lights during the long year of his treatments, recalling so many hikes and bicycle trips with such a good friend. He never complained, not once, even privately to his wife, Marty, she told me. Upon receiving word from his doctor that the cancer was terminal, Bill offered a one-word assessment: *Rats*. I celebrated Holy Communion with Bill at his home a few days before he died, the only time I've ever offered the blood of Christ through a medicine dropper.

I was asked to help at Bill's funeral with our bishop, Richard, and Bill's brother, John, a professor of systematic theology at our Lutheran seminary in Philadelphia. The service at Muhlenberg

Lutheran in Harrisonburg, Virginia, was packed, about six hundred people. A local children's choir (including Bill's two daughters, not yet teenagers) sang a beautiful anthem. Grieving, I could hardly squeak out notes for the opening hymn and later would only be able to hand certain friends the eucharistic bread, wordlessly, unable to croak out "given for you." And here were two beautiful daughters singing their hearts out before hundreds.

The crowd for the funeral was like something from the Day of Pentecost in the book of Acts. Bill decided on ordination years after seminary, as it turned out, serving a small congregation in the Shenandoah Valley in addition to his duties as a full-time park ranger. So, assembled that day was a large cadre of pastors from all over the Virginia Synod, robed with vibrant stoles. And also dozens of park service rangers from across the country, in dark green or tan uniforms, arriving from several states to honor a fallen friend. And more Mennonite couples than I could count, dressed in their traditional clothing, revealing a way of life that was also passing away with time. Bill's spouse, Marty, was a midwife in the area who had delivered hundreds of children in the valley, including many little Mennonites, also in attendance. Also present were so many friends and young couples and relatives from near and far. Bill was only forty-four when he died. It was a colorful and diverse funeral congregation like no other I've ever seen.

John, Bill's brother, rose to speak. Robed and wearing hiking boots, John placed a full Nalgene water bottle on the pulpit before offering a short prayer. He spoke lovingly of his brother, describing several of their favorite hikes and how they would "honor the view" by pouring "a libation" of spring water from their bottles over a precipice to rocks far below. John then referred to a stained-glass window, off to his right, featuring Pastor Peter Muhlenberg who, at the dawn of the Revolutionary War, tore off his clerical robe, revealing a soldier's uniform. Muhlenberg, echoing Ecclesiastes 3, famously said, "There is a time to pray and a time to fight, and that time has come now!" And off he went to war. A decaled facsimile of this scene was once featured on police cars in nearby Woodstock, Virginia.

While telling the Muhlenberg story, John slowly began to remove his own clerical robe. I had no idea what he was doing and have never (before or since) seen a pastor disrobe during a funeral.

John grabbed the water bottle off the pulpit and started running in his clomping boots up through the center aisle of a gawking congregation. Under his robe, John was wearing a pair of Bill's tattered hiking shorts and one of his brother's old T-shirts. I recognized both shorts and shirt. The shorts were somewhat famous. Bill once knelt at the communion rail in seminary while wearing them, prompting a fuming response from a North Carolina Synod bishop in attendance that Thursday evening who demanded the institution of a chapel dress code at a board meeting the next afternoon. The bishop bellowed at that meeting, "I could see that boy's balls hanging out at communion!" Which became an oft-told stretch of the truth, but the shorts were indeed a bit racy.

John ran with his long and bare legs. Six hundred heads turned. At the head of the center aisle, he stopped at the baptismal font, that ancient spring, allowed several beats of silence, and poured the contents of the bottle into the old life-giving vessel, shouting the words, "This water, Bill, has shaped your whole life as a disciple, and I honor the view that Christ has given you these forty-four years!"

Such an echoing silence after John's proclamation in that large church; no one hardly breathed. John's words partly explain why I could hardly speak several minutes later, passing out the body of Christ through tears.

✶

Bill had plenty of blood kin at his funeral that day, those who shared his wit and intelligence, his past and his last name, in a long and colorful genealogical line. But I've come to believe that his baptismal connection to so many gathered mourners was an even more powerful determinant in how he looked at life and shaped the time that filled his relatively brief days on the planet. His life was marked with joy, such an authentic wonder concerning the gift of a shared and intricate creation, and an ability to place even a terminal illness in sacramental perspective. His brother had it right as he poured water into that old Harrisonburg font. Bill had already died with Christ in baptism. His subsequent days were spent splashing around in God's grace and forgiveness, seeing through the lens of resurrection on this side of the grave. The font was both his tomb (Col. 3:3) and his womb (Rom. 6:4); Bill was reborn into an ancient family of water-kin, all marked with the cross of Christ forever.

Baptism can interrupt and usurp my (anyone's) understandable fixation upon relatives from the past and their respective actions, illnesses, and passed-on proclivities. The wonderful conversion story of a blemished Ethiopian eunuch and his baptism on the Gaza wilderness road is situated in the book of Acts (8:26–40) just before Paul's remarkable conversion on the road to Damascus. Both stories describe trading one family for another and suggest how the Holy Spirit's sacramental intervention in one's life recasts one's days in a surpassingly broad ecclesiastical genealogy in the long line of saints and sinners known as the church. "The church," wrote Tertullian (160–after 220), hailing from Carthage in North Africa, not far from the Ethiopian's homeland, "grows not from the loins of the people but by the waters of baptism."

Before retirement, when I used to teach confirmation, our church middle-school kids loved to hear me explain what a eunuch is. A eunuch was hired by the queen to protect her treasury. He was different, altered for political reasons, a trusted part of the queen's inner circle because he was no sexual threat. He gave up his own jewels to guard the queen's. (Sorry about that.)

Bouncing along in the chariot that day on the wilderness road, reading the Bible, this odd man from Africa was drawn to a passage from Isaiah. Why was he reading from Isaiah? Maybe relying on the old index-finger Bible guide? Or maybe this eunuch was drawn to Isaiah because he saw himself there. "Who can describe his generation?" the prophet asks. "For his life is taken away from the earth" (Acts 8:33, quoting Isa. 53:8).

A eunuch had no family through marriage and no foreseeable hope of one. On top of that, the same Bible this man was reading clearly states, rather graphically, that "no one whose testicles are crushed or whose penis is cut off shall be admitted to the assembly of the LORD" (Deut. 23:1).[1] My confirmation kids also enjoyed finding that nugget in their Bibles.

Acts reports that this altered Ethiopian had traveled to Jerusalem in order to worship there, but it's possible that this damaged African had been turned away because his plumbing, so to speak, was not kosher. I'm not really sure how ushers checked this sort of thing at the door, but eunuchs were not welcome in God's house. This man was clearly an outsider with no progeny, no lineage—he simply did not fit in.

The story reports that the Holy Spirit prompts Philip to get up, go to a certain road in the middle of nowhere, and enter a specific chariot. I truly suspect that this is the Holy Spirit's idea, not Philip's. Unlike Saint Paul, a single man who had time to run all over the wide world, Philip is a family man. He had "four unmarried daughters who had the gift of prophecy" (Acts 21:9). Their home life must have been interesting. I'm guessing that if Philip was calling the shots, he'd stay at home and tend to his "real" family. Philip would probably not be out on that desert road if left to him.

The new family described in this story is never our idea. Most people establish family boundaries with blood and name. God dreams of boundaries obliterated by water. Philip climbs in the chariot and becomes a confirmation teacher.

The chariot arrives at a roadside pool. "Look, here is water! What's to stop me from being baptized into this new family?" asks the eunuch (8:37, trans. FGH). A heck of a lot, actually—ethnicity, homeland, the fact that he was damaged goods. Even the Bible included a prohibition.

An outsider, cut off from any hope of family, is welcomed in. And if you miss the message here, Saint Paul's conversion immediately follows. A eunuch gets in. And then a former persecutor of Christians gets in. They even let me in.

The British poet Philip Larkin (1922–1985) penned a powerful poem with baptismal themes titled "Water." The second stanza suggests that churchgoing should involve "a fording to dry, different clothes." In the fourth stanza, the poet raises a glass of water in the east, "where any-angled light would congregate endlessly."

This baptism of a once-excluded man (and the subsequent dousing of another improbable convert who once imprisoned and tortured people he would eventually call brothers and sisters) completely scrambles a Christian's perception of who is "kin" and radically reframes traditional notions of genealogy, family, and ancestry with "any-angled light" refracting through water that, with my friend Bill, honors a whole new view of the world into which followers of Jesus are reborn. The church has forded an ancient river necessitating a change of garment: "As God's chosen ones, holy and beloved, clothe yourselves with compassion, kindness, humility, meekness, and patience. . . . Above all, clothe yourselves with love, which binds everything together in perfect harmony" (Col. 3:12, 14). New duds, a new wardrobe that changes everything.

*

There's a wonderfully descriptive story near the end of Ezekiel, a rather bizarre book filled with acted-out oracles, rich imagery, and vivid visions including cooking with human dung, bizarre flying wheels, and a valley of dry bones. The book is generally set in the period just after Judah has been taken into exile in Babylonia and, like other apocalyptic books, attempts to make sense of the suffering that has befallen God's people. Some Jewish traditions forbid the reading of the book by anyone under the age of thirty. It's consistently graphic and odd but also quite compelling.

The vision in Ezekiel 47, located in the penultimate chapter, is milder (and more beautiful) than most of the others in the book and suggests the source of renewal and hope in faithful worship that centers upon and flows from the temple.

A holy guide accompanies Ezekiel to the entrance of the temple (47:1). This guide has been with our prophetic friend for quite a while, reminding Ezekiel of certain tasks that priests (whose corruption is exposed throughout the book) should faithfully tend to. Ezekiel is shown water whose hidden source begins beneath the temple and flows outward, deepening and expanding far downstream. The water flows into the surrounding community, and Ezekiel feels it tickle his ankles and knees until the stream becomes a river so deep that he cannot cross it (47:3–5).

Now on the bank of the deep river, Ezekiel notices healthy trees on both sides of the waterway. This is quite an enlivening body of water whose theological source (the temple, faithful worship) is not lost on our hero. Ezekiel sees appreciably further downstream in the vision and realizes the river makes fresh even "the sea of stagnant waters" (47:8), better known as the Dead Sea. The holy guide then makes an incredible claim: "everything will live where the river goes" (47:9).

I've used this story occasionally at funerals, particularly with saints of the church whose entire lives have been powerfully centered in the gift of baptism, its healing waters beginning at a certain font but always flowing outward into the community, deepening and refreshing relationships, shaping responses to justice issues, and overcoming crippling fear, even the fear of death.

This ancient story from Ezekiel, sacramentally suggestive, shapes the stories of those who search for relatives (from whom they may feel a bit exiled) in their genealogical past. I'm especially thinking of three friends who've recently located relatives through DNA saliva tests—a half brother in Germany who located my friend decades after their common father served in the military there; a birth father in Florida who happily discovered a daughter (my friend, adopted as a little girl) whom he did not know even existed until they learned of each other through the test; and a third friend whose DNA reconnection story I'll tell now in some detail (with her permission).

Christie[2] grew up in the rural Northeast in a family with four siblings and two parents; her childhood was mostly normal until it wasn't. Her father, a college professor, abruptly moved out after an affair with one of his students. A baby was born from that union. Christie's family was devastated. Her mother, suddenly single, struggled to make ends meet on one salary. It was a tough time. Her father cut off contact with the family.

Bizarrely, Christie (and the surrounding community) learned that her father took the baby one night and fled south, just the two of them. No one knew where or exactly why. The mother of the baby was frantic. Police became involved. The father and the baby boy seemingly vanished. No word, no news. No one—Christie's family, the mother of the baby, the police—knew what became of the fleeing father and this child. Christie worried about a possible mental health breakdown her father may have experienced and was prone to. Decades passed.

Christie's brother, Tom, now an adult living in a southern state, took a DNA test and checked the box inviting contact if any matches surfaced. Weeks later, Tom received a message from someone also inviting contact. The man named Rich, incredibly, lived only four miles away. The two men met for coffee.

Rich brought along a newspaper story, faded and frayed, describing a baby left in a box in the vestibule of a Methodist church, found by the smiling church janitor who was holding the baby in the story's photo. A diaper was in the box and no information. Not a note, nothing. It was hard to place this child (eventually adopted by a loving family) who seemingly materialized from air in that church with no identifying details, no past connection to anyone, as if he dropped out of heaven from God. Adding to these oddities, we all learned much later that our seminary classmate's father, a policeman, led the local investigation of this abandoned baby, a pre-Internet investigation that produced no leads.

Rich and Tom talked about a lot of things that day after connecting all the dots. Phone calls were placed and other meetings arranged with the siblings. Rich's birth mother, who'd started a new life, did not desire contact. Christie's father somehow escaped legal responsibility or detection in another state and died alone.

I phoned Christie the other day to ask about a few details and reaffirm her permission to share the story. "We knew there was someone, somewhere out there. We had no idea how he might be doing after my dad went off the rails."

We talked about the various subsequent meetings between Rich and her siblings, joyful and awkward at the same time. Christie described Rich's adoptive family, his mom and dad; what great and caring people they were.

"The body of Christ is powerfully present in this situation," she said, "with this faithful adoptive couple. My mom would have been thrilled, way back when, to know this baby was placed in a loving family. She took refugees into her home at one point when we were older. With church, even when people screw up, like my dad did, faithful people step forward. With a community of friends and faith, you're supported. Love makes it okay." Over the phone, miles apart, we were both crying.

We hung up and I thought of Ezekiel and the source of that old spring, deepening and widening as it flowed out the door, downstream.

"Everything will live where the river goes."

✶

When our three children were young, we used to depart our home in southwest Virginia, cross a couple of state lines over tall mountains, and meet their South Carolina cousins halfway in the small town of Mars Hill, North Carolina.

Much later, I learned that this site of a historic North Carolina college with a Baptist history probably derived its name from the "Areopagus" mentioned in Acts 17:22, in English called Mars Hill, part of the landscape encountered by Saint Paul as he wandered around Athens, observing shrines to a number of local gods. The narrator for this section of Acts reports that "all the Athenians and the foreigners living there would spend their time in nothing but telling or hearing something new" (17:21). Paul's life was threatened in two previous towns (Thessalonica and Beroea), but in Athens, standing in front of Mars Hill, he was mostly met with indifference and shrugs when he shared good news about the resurrection of the dead and a new family created by Christ in baptism.

We once arrived in Mars Hill well before the cousins from South Carolina and had a bit of time. Our meeting place overlooked a winding four-lane highway. From that lofty perch, we could sometimes pick out their car approaching from the south, creating excitement and even more anticipation for greeting relatives we hadn't seen in months.

My son Lukas, then seven, and I decided to walk downhill on a faint path and soon encountered an old overgrown cemetery with tipped stones and almost illegible inscriptions. The cemetery was not visible from above or below its rectangular plot of land once lovingly carved out of the hillside.

Lukas knelt in front of two small markers, and I joined him there in the grass and weeds. He traced the dates with his finger in fading afternoon light, and I watched him do the math in his mind, eyes widening, as he computed the number of years straddling the hyphen separating birth and death.

"They were only kids," he said, "about my age." We spoke their first names aloud, wondering how they may have died.

*

I come from a family filled with unusual characters, probably a lot like yours in its sometimes bizarre twists and turns, odd incidents and accidents, including premature deaths. My younger brother died of brain cancer not many years ago. I miss him intensely, still tracing the years in my mind bracketing his own hyphen between life . . . and what? What sort of new existence awaits any of us on the other side of the grave?

I invite you to distrust anyone who claims to know about such an existence in intimate detail. The Bible points to an afterlife but is often unusually restrained concerning the furniture and topography of such a place, such an existence. For Christians, descriptions of life in the kingdom, centering upon the radical teachings of Jesus, suggest that such an existence begins now for the baptized, its future permutations a clear continuance of what Jesus inaugurated in his earthly life and ministry. I often wonder what a plurality of Christians in the United States, many bent on exclusion and division in our recent national election, really thinks "heaven" will be like when all God's people assemble for a future feast.

I'm writing these words in the darkening days of November, the season of melancholy for many—leaves falling, giving way to gravity and frost; colorful pathways, transient, raked away like a fleeting rainbow.

I watch the leaves fall and am reminded of a film based upon the James Joyce short story "The Dead," where the main character stands at a second-story window, watching the snow fall. He has just left a family reunion in Ireland and knows that he will never see some of his family members ever again. Knows that they will not live another year. The falling snow reminds him of the many people he has known and loved who have died not only in his lifetime but also back through Ireland's past. The camera sweeps to cemetery after cemetery around the country. The snow relentlessly falls on all the grave markers. He wonders about his own place in the vastness of space and time.

Annie Dillard wonders about her own mortality:

> Since sand and dirt pile up on everything, why does [the world] look fresh for each new crowd? As natural and human debris raises the continents, vegetation grows on the piles. It is all a stage set—we know this—a temporary stage on top of many layers of stages, but every year . . . a new crop of sand, grass, and tree leaves freshens the set and perfects the illusion that ours is the new and urgent world now. . . . In every arable soil in the world we grow grain over tombs. . . . Living things from hyenas to bacteria whisk the dead away like stagehands hustling props between scenes.[3]

The Sadducees once approached Jesus with a trick question, a first-century knock-knock joke meant to embarrass the man and make him squirm (Luke 20:27–40). "Hey, Jesus," we imagine them saying. "Have you ever heard the one about the woman who married seven brothers? Each of them in turn kicked the bucket and left her childless. Tell us, O Wise One. In heaven, whose wife will she be? She was married to all of them." Many flying elbows into ribs, all around. The musical *Seven Brides for Seven Brothers* comes to mind. The Sadducees come to Jesus and want to know about seven brothers and just one bride. Who "gets her" in the resurrection, Jesus?

There is no break in the text, but I imagine Jesus let that question sink in a while. He let it sit there long enough to make the adolescent questioners a little nervous about the silence that ensued.

Even though these funny boys bring Jesus a preposterous question, the same question raises our own sense of natural curiosity about the afterlife. In what Jesus calls "that age," will we know each other? How will husbands and wives relate? Will I get to talk to Martin Luther? What will it be like there? How will we live? I have an amusing A-type friend who has a hard time sitting still. "I'll need something to do in heaven. I need a task!" These aren't bad questions to ask in November with the leaves piling up outside.

"In that age," Jesus says, people "neither marry nor are given in marriage. Indeed they cannot die anymore, because they are like angels and are children of God, being children of the resurrection" (20:35-36).

In the coming age, nobody will "have" anybody else. All relations will be changed. People will not "have" a wife or husband or partner. Couples will not "have" children, but together the celestial assembly will be "children of the resurrection." There will be no earthly family groupings in the coming age, says Jesus, only the family of God.

I'm not sure whether these words of Jesus make any November easier or harder. His answer pushes me yet another step down the road toward considering the big biblical questions: Who *is* my family? Who *is* my neighbor? Who *is* my next of kin?

The Bible doesn't spend much time indulging our very natural and normal questions about heaven. There's much we cannot know. But this much seems to be crystal clear: heaven signals the end of "having"—having children, a spouse, an earthly family. And if that's true, several questions are in order. How does such a coming reality shape the way we now live? How do Jesus's words affect our most intimate relationships in these days? What *is* a family anyway, and how should it function in this world given a coming age when we are all God's children?

It's natural to think of those whom we have loved, now gone. Will I know them? Will I see them again? Will we ever be together? Christ says yes. But the relationship will be different, changed.

In Christ, it is changing now. Disciples follow the One who raises "children of the resurrection" on both sides of the grave, born anew in every time and place.

And for those who see past the falling leaves, it means the end of "having," the end of sharp distinctions defined by name and genealogy, the end of limiting our love or allowing a past to completely define us.

*

They're all here—in my imagination, my waking days, my dreams of a new future.

Sheriff Frank and Will who was hanged. Bill on the trail at an old spring. My brother, Lee, who died young. Aunt Eulie and her caretakers near Memphis. Scores of parishioners who meant much to me. Mom and Dad. My wife's loving parents. All my teachers; so many mentors. The long roll of singing saints, marked with the cross of Christ forever in baptism.

Lukas and I climbed back up the hill from the overgrown cemetery in Mars Hill late that afternoon. We settled into a grassy spot with the rest of the family, sipping soft drinks and watching the approaching traffic down below on the four-lane, anticipating a sweet reunion with relatives from the south. Headlights were starting to come on in the beautiful last light of the day, blinking like fireflies.

Surrounded by death, steeped in centuries of history marked with stories of loss and love, we all look into the far distance, waiting for a long-anticipated reunion.

Watching, longing for the promised light ever coming toward us.

Chapter 7

OUR SPECK OF LIFE, OUR TICK OF TIME

"The unfolding of your words gives light."

—*Psalm 119:130*

"How small our span of life, O God, our years from birth to death:
A single beat within the heart, the catching of a breath. . . .
And yet our speck of life is spanned by your infinity;
Our tick of time on earth is caught in your eternity."

—*Herman G. Stuempfle Jr. (1923–2007),*
"How Small Our Span of Life,"
Evangelical Lutheran Worship *hymn #636*

I was reading the story of Zacchaeus (Luke 19:1–10) recently, late in the church year, and was reminded of an interesting interpretive twist affirmed by several early church commentators. The pronoun at the end of the third verse in this familiar story (in English and Greek) is provocatively ambiguous. The tax man, trying to get a glimpse of Jesus, fails on his first viewing attempt because of the large crowd. He then shimmies up a famous sycamore tree for a better view. The text says the climb occurred "because he was short in stature" (19:3). But here's the delightful interpretive dilemma. Exactly *who* was short in stature?

Take a look at the story and read it slowly. A compelling case can be made that *Jesus* (not Zacchaeus) was difficult to see because of his relatively short height, especially when surrounded by a crowd in a town like Jericho. With this shift in pronoun perspective, Zacchaeus—the shady tax collector, perhaps seeking a new start in life—climbs a tree to get a better look at the wee teacher who is all but invisible at ground level, swallowed by folk hanging on his every word.

If this is true, that Jesus (not Zacchaeus) is the fairly short man requiring a potential convert's sycamore climb to properly absorb life-changing words, then lots of Bible images explode in my imagination beyond the possibility of the Lord of Heaven and Earth resembling a sassy Danny DeVito.

It may explain how Jesus was consistently able to hide from enemies who wanted him dead. It may suggest why Judas needed to kiss and identify a surprising troublemaker when soldiers may have been expecting a more formidable and much taller enemy. And it certainly fits the proclivities of God whose thoughts are not ours (Isa. 55:8) and who consistently chooses unexpected venues for revelation, including an unlikely Bethlehem barn.

The Bible is an enchantingly bizarre library of bound books. The evening news comes at us fast and furiously and includes distracting zippy commercials. The Bible requires the serious reader to slow down, *way down*, to unveil its surprising truth.

This is not an easy enterprise for a distracted nation (and church) like ours. Reading Scripture is not an easy "express insight" enterprise. Truth in the Bible is often mined, percolated, sifted, and examined from multiple angles.

A daily reader of the Bible for over three decades, I'm now convinced such sifting is an on-purpose recurring *intention* authored by the surprising and often comedic guile of the Holy Spirit, who inspired its many writers. I'm not talking about intentional obfuscation, so fuzzy that only academics can cipher the Bible's "true" meaning. I am saying that Bible interpretation will be at least as mind-bending as a challenging board game, requiring patience, attention, creative thinking, even risk.

There is a great scene in the movie *Smoke* (1995), set in New York City. A tobacco shop owner named Auggie (Harvey Keitel) has the curious habit of snapping a photograph outside his shop each morning at the exact same time. Each day of the year, precisely at the same time, in all sorts of weather, he never misses. Auggie has dozens of albums with these photos, covering decades of time.

One night in his apartment, Auggie shows the albums to his writer friend, Paul (William Hurt), who is suffering from writer's block after an accident. Paul flips through the album pages quickly, laughs, and says, "They're all the same."

Auggie begins to gather up his photos, a bit offended. "No, you're missing it. You'll miss the point if you look at them that way. You'll miss the people. All these people who have come to my little corner in this little part of the world. And you'll miss the light. How the earth turns at different times of the year. How the sun hits my corner at a different angle in the spring from the fall. You may as well not look at them if you're gonna go that fast."

Wise pastors and church leaders will adopt the thinking of Auggie as they plan ministries introducing new adult Christians to the power and depth of the Bible. The church's book is not filled with stories at which a mature Christian simply glances.

It took me a while, for example, to discover that Jesus is often something of a tease in the Gospels. This is not initially apparent in examining the life of a man who seems utterly serious and offers no recorded scene of laughter. Jesus, however, knew all about humor and had impeccable timing.

Cleopas and an unnamed friend walk away from Jerusalem, apparently punting on the early church community after the crucifixion of Jesus. "We had hoped that he was the one to redeem Israel" (Luke 24:21). A third man appears and walks along, seemingly unaware of the sadness that's recently occurred on a hill outside the city. Stunned, Cleopas is curt with the clueless newcomer: "Are you the only stranger in Jerusalem unaware of these things?"

Perhaps Jesus waits a few seconds to answer. But take a moment to sound out his reply (24:19) and let it sink in. "*What things?*" Two words, one small question. Seinfeld couldn't have staged it better.

It also took me a while to notice tiny bits of Bible data that often unlock new worlds of interpretation. Consider Peter's speech to gathered believers just before Pentecost in the first-century equivalent of the church announcement period. Peter is explaining the treachery of Judas and his grisly demise (Acts 1:15–19). The original Greek includes no punctuation. But a slow interpretive guess on the boundaries of Peter's speech reveals fascinating possibilities. The NRSV interrupts Peter's words after verse 17 and then includes a couple of graphic parenthetical sentences describing Judas's bowels, a PG-13 depiction of the traitor's death.

Interestingly, the Revised Standard Version (RSV) chooses to include the bowel-gushing data within Peter's speech; a rather explicit announcement by the presiding minister in the gathered assembly offered with no editorial screen.

Which punctuation choice does the patient interpreter make? Personally, I like the unsanitized RSV approach, which might lead to more transparent honesty on Sunday mornings for clergy like me who sometimes tend to protect parishioners from the nitty-gritty details of church life.

But the main point: even something as small as punctuation choice matters in the slow percolation and mining of biblical truth.

My wife and I once vacationed with another couple on Smith Mountain Lake in Virginia. They brought a competitive board game called Wingspan that we played one rainy day. The game teaches avian habits and requires a mindful balancing of eggs, food tokens, and bird cards. Our friends patiently explained the rules. We finished playing and I had to lie down on the floor for a nap. The game is brain taxing, and mine was toast. I suspect one must play Wingspan multiple times to get any good at it.

After many years of reading and wondering, I've decided the Bible works in a somewhat similar way, requiring our best thinking and prayerful discernment over distilled, percolated time. The Bible is not meant to be easy. (Neither were your best teachers.) Like faithful genealogical work, bits of bread dropped teasingly along a winding path, the Bible can lead to locked doors and frustrating turns down unexpected forks in the road. Over steeped time, however, in the patient sifting of detail and surprise, the church gains measured insight and holy wisdom.

Zacchaeus once went out of his way and patiently climbed a tree to get a glimpse of Jesus, perhaps through tangled branches. It made all the difference.[1]

*

Daniel Mason's ambitious and fascinating novel *North Woods* describes various residents of a single house in rural New England over centuries of time. The house changes shape through the years, as do the pasture, orchards, and surrounding woods. I read the novel and came away with a better respect for the holy passage of time in my own neighborhood in upstate South Carolina, wondering about its previous residents and how my nearby creek (where I still search for elusive fish) may have entertained or nourished a parade of occupants of this land whose remnants have now intermingled with the other side of the soil. Mason writes near the end of the book about "the grand cinema of the forest's passage."

> Here Pocumtuc men and women cultivated fields along the river floodplain. Here the beech and oak rose slowly in the shade of nurse trees. Here the birch shot up after the King's men took pine to raise as masts over their ships. . . . It was as if the past were written everywhere upon the land. In the size of stones found in the snaking walls, which told whether the land was used for crop or pasture. In the rotted hemlock

> that registered its ghost beneath the stilted roots of silver birch. The Eastern white pine that owed its bifurcated form to the marauding of a weevil in its sapling-hood. The many-fingered trunks that testified to browsing deer long dead.[2]

Genealogical insight—like reading the Bible (dense with intrigue and often curious plots), or sifting the geography of a piece of land and its residents over measured time—may rest upon very small details that only lead to partial (but important) intuitive insight about the motivations and moods of our forebears. I don't know a whole lot about my great-grandfather, Sheriff Frank, but I do know that his gaze still follows me around my living room, convincing me that his odd and tragic inheritance has shaped my life in ways I'm unable to fully articulate. But God has used this tragic inheritance to form me into the pastor, father, husband, and friend that I am today, complete with flaws, regrets, gifts, and hope. Nor do I know all I'd like to know about my great-aunt Eulie, but I've pieced together enough of her life to know her story still swims through my complicated brain chemistry and sometimes affects melancholy days, dark periods, but also generates weird and fun ideas and unusual directions.

We are all shaped by a complicated and astonishing genetic inheritance. It is indeed amazing and ponderous that any of us almost did not make our planetary debut; that any of us almost *wasn't*. Had a few minute details from the past been tinkered with, I would not be writing these words nor would you be reading them. Like the forest surrounding that centuries-old house in Daniel Mason's novel, any of us (with limits, of course) can peel back layers of time and examine the incidents, scars, chance, providence, good fortune, divine intention, love, and maybe luck that brought any of us to this day, this moment.

How we think about all this—our speck of life, our tick of time, as hymn writer Herman Stuempfle puts it—matters greatly and shapes how we spend our days, how we think about the mind of God who brought such diverse people into being, and how we seek to honor God's deep desire for justice and grace in a world broken by sin and deep division. "The truth turns into a story when it grows old," writes Niall Williams. "We all become stories in the end."[3] Our search for meaning in the old stories of those who've preceded (and still shape) us is primarily a search for truth that God attempts to embody in my life and yours, also revealed in the stories people might tell about any of us decades or centuries hence.

This search for truth and meaning will certainly include frustrating limits warned about in the Bible, specifically by Qoheleth,[4] the wise (and sometimes jaded) preacher from the book of Ecclesiastes: "I have seen the business that God has given to everyone to be busy with. He has made everything suitable for its time; moreover he has put a sense of past and future into their minds, yet they cannot find out what God has done from the beginning to the end" (3:10–11). Presumably, it's important to be "busy" with the "business" described in the book you're presently holding. The search you've embarked upon finds its genesis not just in curiosity but also in biblical affirmation. But roadblocks and limited insight will invariably litter the path of anyone who chooses to embark upon a genealogical search. Knowing this, the preacher suggests there is "nothing better" than enjoyment and happiness in the present life (3:12), as far as both are possible as the search reaches its limits.

Many, of course, have objected to this advice, unable to find happiness or joy in genealogical profundities—notably Job, whose frustration with God simmers over to anger in a couple verses I've always loved. Here Job is replying to his friend Bildad, who suggests that Job's problems in his search for meaning reside in some secret sin from the distant past requiring repentance. Job listens to his friend but finally throws his hands up in exasperation with God:

> "Look, he passes by me, and I do not see him;
> he moves on, but I do not perceive him.
> He snatches away; who can stop him?
> Who will say to him, 'What are you doing?' . . .
> There is no umpire between us,
> who might lay his hand on us both."
>
> (Job 9:11–12, 33)

Centuries later, Saint Paul suggests that "crushed and perplexed" people like us (recalling, at times, our predecessor in suffering, Job)—fragile "clay jars" that we are, often feeling umpire-less, void of divine meaning and insight, passed over by God—will not ultimately arrive at despair, "carrying in the body the death of Jesus, so that the life of Jesus may also be made visible in our bodies" (see 2 Cor. 4:7–12). A portable (and baptismal) truth to take on the road as you search. For Christians, the "umpire" we seek is Jesus. Then this: "So we do not lose heart. Even though our outer nature is wasting away, our inner nature is being renewed day by day. For this slight momentary affliction is preparing us for an eternal weight of glory beyond all measure, because we look not at what can be seen but at what cannot be seen; for what can be seen is temporary, but what cannot be seen is eternal" (2 Cor. 4:16–18).

My understanding of the line in the Apostles' Creed concerning a belief "in the communion of saints" certainly involves peering toward what "cannot be seen" in both directions—back toward the unseen past and forward toward an unseen future. I'm convinced that a genealogical search, shaped by centuries-old biblical tradition, does indeed daily assist in renewing "our inner nature," even as aging bodies like mine continue to "waste away."

The two-year daily lectionary that my wife and I follow from *Lutheran Book of Worship* just began the calendar new year with a series of passages that concluded with a famous verse from the book of Hebrews: "Therefore, since we are surrounded by so great a cloud of witnesses, let us also lay aside every weight and sin that clings so closely, and let us run with perseverance the race that is set before us" (12:1). I love this verse, but it's important to explore the "therefore" that prompts such a bold invitation toward theological tenacity.

Chapter 11 includes an impressive list of characters and spiritual forebears, including Abraham—who embarked on a journey "not knowing where he was going" (11:8), not a bad metaphor for the journey described in this book—Moses, Rahab (one of the female ancestors in Jesus's genealogy, please recall), Gideon, Samson, David, and a host of others whose exploits and challenges are summarized in breathtaking fashion:

> who through faith conquered kingdoms, administered justice, obtained promises, shut the mouths of lions, quenched raging fire, escaped the edge of the sword, won strength out of weakness, became mighty in war, put foreign enemies to flight. Women received their dead by resurrection. Others were tortured, refusing to accept release, in order to obtain a better resurrection. Others suffered mocking and flogging, and even chains and imprisonment. They were stoned to death, they were sawn in two, they were killed by the sword; they went about in skins of sheep and goats, destitute, persecuted, tormented—of whom the world was not worthy. They wandered in deserts and mountains, and in caves and holes in the ground. (Heb. 11:32–38)

It is forebears like these, blood kin and baptismal kin, "the great cloud of witnesses," who surround us and, I daresay, cheer on their descendants from an unseen vantage point. I feel such encouragement from the communion of saints on many days, usually when looking back and ahead in genealogical ponderings similar to those we've encountered in these pages.

I'm holding an old picture of Aunt Eulie that I found the other day. She looks to be in her late teenage years; the photo is perhaps taken just before she boarded a train for her freshman year at SMU in Dallas. A profile perspective, professionally crafted, in which she is looking down and away from the viewer with serious eyes, barenecked with some sort of flimsy chiffon material over her shoulders; pursed lips with just a mere hint of a smile. She seems deep in thought, maybe wondering about some problem. Only her head and shoulders are shown, offering a disembodied appearance; this was a popular portrait perspective in the early twentieth-century but also one that fits what I know about her, someone who undoubtedly spent a lot of time in her head. As do I, it turns out, in mine.

I cannot claim to really know, but I like to think that Eulie is indeed cheering on descendants like me from her perspective among the cloud of witnesses, cheering on scientists and researchers who painstakingly explore the vicissitudes of the human mind and our complex brain circuitry. "The brain has billions of interconnected neurons," writes Jonathan Rosen, commenting upon recent discoveries. "Schizophrenia doesn't attack a single region but affects networks connecting multiple parts of the brain, including those involved with our ability to imagine things that don't yet exist, along with our ability to believe in what we imagine. In that regard, it is the most human of disorders, a reminder of how remarkable our minds are. It's like the Tin Man realizing he has a heart because it's breaking."[5]

I see in my mind's eye several minutes of drone footage I discovered online. The drone provides interesting angles from outside (high above, then swooping, pausing, hovering, like an interested hummingbird) the abandoned Western State Hospital in Bolivar that opened in 1889. It shows the imposing entrance with old stairs and heavy double doors; a beautiful tiled roof, severely pitched in spots, in need of repair; an open window on the third floor, providing a peek into an empty hallway filled with light from the setting sun; a long approach lane lined with old and massive trees, ending at a dry fountain; an expansive view of the Tennessee hills protecting the old building, perched on an elevated high point surrounded by open fields.

Lots of suffering occurred within the walls of the state hospital that the drone cannot record. Some of the suffering was inherited genetically; some suffering was inflicted experimentally by flawed but well-intentioned physicians; some suffering was hatched knowingly by a warped social worker and her accomplices.

I'd love to know what Eulie was thinking in that old picture from her late teenage years, if she had any idea at all what her emerging confused thoughts meant. I'd love to know more about what prompted my grandfather to never speak about his sister for all those decades or even reveal Eulie's existence to his own daughters. I wish I hadn't been so distracted with my own vocation and young family that I failed to ask Mom what it was like to meet Eulie at Western State for the first time after not knowing her aunt was even in the world. But I mostly trust that God has mended what was broken in Eulie, and is mending what's broken in us all.

*

I'm staring this morning at a photo of a two-story house, built in 1900, on Corban Street in downtown Concord, North Carolina, just a block or so from Saint James Lutheran Church. Zillow tells me that the house is a triplex now, renovated several times for various occupants since Sheriff Frank and Agnes raised a young family within its fairly new walls, still whispering stories of a gallows nearby and the December fate of Will Brown almost 120 years ago. I squint through the windows and try to imagine Aggie sewing the gallows hood and Frank poring over Luther's *Small Catechism* by a small fire kindled near a Christmas tree. I see young well-scrubbed boys walking to church with their parents, who greet assembling neighbors, enter the hush of the sanctuary, and kneel inside Saint James for confession followed by biblical counsel and inspired hymn singing. And I hear the trapdoor give way just before noon, exactly a week before the famous nativity, with thousands milling about in the town square, a breaking neck echoing over time.

According to the front page of the local newspaper, Will "received his friends and a large number of curious white people" at the jail that morning, "to tell the doomed man goodbye."[6] A hymn was sung before the procession to the gallows commenced: "Blest Be the Tie That Binds."

Curious white people—Christians, predominately Lutherans, who were attracted as to a circus sideshow to see the hanging of a man whose accuser could not initially identify him.

The house on Corban Street undoubtedly heard quiet conversations about the hanging in weeks and months to come, both on the front porch with friends and between the young sheriff and his wife. I like to think that "justice" and "grace" were among the words that swam around below the bedroom ceiling during those dark and maybe sleepless late nights. Sheriff Frank owned a number of rental properties in later years. According to my mother: "Most of the tenants were black and Frank liked to play checkers with them. It is thought that he must not have lost too heavily as he would come home late in a very happy mood."[7]

*

"Under Jocassee,"[8] one of my favorite poems written by my friend Ron Rash, invites the reader to rent a boat on a warm summer morning and hug the western shoreline of Lake Jocassee (not far from where I live in upstate South Carolina) until arriving at the cove that was once Horsepasture River, still flowing below the surface of the lake that was formed by a Duke Power dam in 1973. Signs of former mountain communities can still be seen in the clear water depths—graveyards, foundations of barns and houses, even churches with old hymns bubbling to the surface.

The poet invites the reader to cut the motor and drift, to peer far down to the lake bottom and imagine a young woman, early in her marriage as she walks from the barn following chores, singing to herself. She suddenly shivers and stops singing, sensing "something dark has come over her." Even though the day is cloudless, she looks up, believing someone has just crossed over her grave, an old mountain belief linked to unexplained premonition.

Rash returns the boat occupant back to the present, to the lake surface, with the recognition that it's the young woman's grave "you've just passed over." She has sensed me, the reader, above her on the water in the future, mysteriously linked with the past.

Any authentic genealogical search tinted with theological and biblical perspective will pass over a great number of watery graves, sacramentally saturated in baptism, connecting centuries of time. Like you, I am genetically and curiously linked, for better and for worse, to a host of disparate characters and relatives—ranging from Sheriff Frank to Aunt Eulie and many others—and their arresting stories, some details known and others still hidden. But I am also joined by baptism to many other stories to help me make sense of mine, grafted into the Bible's abundant narratives involving water from rock, springs in the desert, and dangerous sea crossings involving escape and liberation.

Some rural congregations, especially those with members who tend to remain in the community their entire lives, observe an old practice that surely gives pause to even the youngest children in the church. After celebrating an ancient liturgy when someone is baptized, the pastor scoops water from the font into a pouring vessel and leads the congregation outside to the church cemetery in procession, the newly baptized at the front, either in parental arms or walking. The assembly stops at the family grave plot where some of the deceased relatives reside in centuries-old graves. After a prayer and a hymn, the carried baptismal water is poured directly on the very gravesite where the just-baptized person will be buried some day in the future. A powerful rite suggesting that death will not have the last say.

And yet, in theological truth, all the dunked or doused have been buried already. "Do you not know that all of us who have been baptized into Christ Jesus were baptized into his death? Therefore we have been buried with him by baptism into death, so that, just as Christ was raised from the dead by the glory of the Father, so we too might walk in newness of life" (Rom. 6:3-4).

Our "unformed substance" (Ps. 139:16)—amazingly known by God when none of our days yet existed—moves through the years across time and space, over many graves and generations, slowly creating and shaping the altogether unique and ponderous person that is you.

NOTES

Introduction

1. Paul Harding, *This Other Eden* (New York: Norton, 2023), 23.

Chapter 1

1. *Evangelical Lutheran Worship* (Minneapolis: Augsburg Fortress, 2006), 104.

2. Judith Shulevitz, "How Marilynne Robinson Reads Scripture," *Atlantic*, March 2024, 94.

3. Sylvia G. Dunstan (1955–1993), "Bless Now, O God, the Journey," in *Evangelical Lutheran Worship*, hymn 326 (verse 1).

4. Oddly, Bathsheba's actual name is not used in the genealogy; more on that later.

5. Both are also named in Matt. 1:3.

6. An unfair coupling of two distinct acts if you ask me, perhaps inflicting unnecessary guilt upon adolescent males for generations to come!

7. "Timnah" is a wordplay on the Hebrew word for "conceal."

8. The NT Greek word for "prostitutes" is *pornai*, from whence we receive the word "pornography."

9. See Josh. 2:18. No husband or children are mentioned in Rahab's list of protected family members.

10. I once heard Tony Campolo (in a sermon) say that "Sons of Thunder" would be an excellent choice for the name of a motorcycle gang, stenciled on the back of their jackets.

11. Joseph Heller, *God Knows* (New York: Knopf, 1984), 192.

Chapter 2

1. Miller Williams, "Beside an Open Grave the Mind of the Young Preacher Comes Almost to Terms," in *Points of Departure* (Urbana: University of Illinois Press, 1995), 29.

2. Providence, literally, means "to see ahead"—"pro" plus "video."

3. Matthew Myer Boulton, "Was My Father Right About Predestination?" *Christian Century*, June 15, 2022, 26. This entire article is excellent and widened my thinking on the controversial word.

4. The closest Jesus comes to judgment "gotcha" in this story is perhaps a bit of sarcasm hidden in his question, "Children, you have no fish, have you?" (21:5).

5. The Hebrew word for "follow" in this famous psalm is also used to describe Pharaoh and his soldiers in hot pursuit of the children of Israel as they flee toward the Red Sea. The implication for the goodness and mercy mentioned in Ps. 23 is that both divine gifts are in constant pursuit of God's people with the intent to catch any of us.

6. The next section of this chapter (in slightly different form) first appeared in my essay "A Weary Prophet: Jeremiah's Vexing Task," *Christian Century*, January 11, 2012, 12–13.

7. Garret Keizer, *The Enigma of Anger: Essays on a Sometimes Deadly Sin* (San Francisco: Jossey-Bass, 2002), 279.

Chapter 3

1. See "Western State Mental Hospital," accessed June 9, 2025, https://abandonedsoutheast.com/2016/11/01/mental-asylum/.

2. Jack El-Hai, *The Lobotomist: A Maverick Medical Genius and His Tragic Quest to Rid the World of Mental Illness* (Hoboken, NJ: Wiley & Sons, 2005).

3. Jamison writes candidly and movingly about her own history and challenges with bipolar disorder and its undeniable genetic link in many family genealogies. Many consider Jamison the world's leading voice on the illness.

4. Jonathan Rosen's book *The Best Minds: A Story of Friendship, Madness, and the Tragedy of Good Intentions* (New York: Penguin Press, 2023), a Pulitzer Prize finalist, is a must-read for anyone who cares about these issues. Rosen's description of his lifelong and brilliant friend who suffers from schizophrenia is both tragic and unforgettable.

5. Frank G. Honeycutt, "Pastor Polar," in *God's Scorekeeper and Other Stories* (Eugene, OR: Cascade, 2019), 54.

6. Kay Redfield Jamison, *An Unquiet Mind: A Memoir of Moods and Madness* (New York: Knopf, 1995), 174.

7. Generally speaking, schizophrenia is a thought disorder that often gives birth to acute suspicion and hallucinatory images. Bipolar disorder primarily affects mood and how one feels.

8. It is also worth noting the odd behaviors of King Saul in First Samuel, who suffered from acute paranoia, bizarre delusions, outsized megalomania, and violent acts of envy, all of which also suggest a man struggling with profound mental illness, perhaps schizophrenia.

9. Jamison, *An Unquiet Mind*, 218.

10. Elyn R. Saks, *The Center Cannot Hold: My Journey Through Madness* (New York: Hachette Books, 2007), 336.

11. See, for example, Paul's concern with "the weak and beggarly elemental spirits" described in Gal. 4:8–11 and his fear that the church might return to them.

12. Heidi Haverkamp, "The Wisdom of Not Knowing," *Christian Century*, April 2024, 65.

13. Jayne Anne Phillips, *Night Watch* (New York: Knopf, 2024), 14.

Chapter 4

1. Feel free to skip over Gen. 38, since we've already examined it in some detail in chapter 1 of this book.

2. The Hebrew word here literally means "evil."

3. Frank G. Honeycutt, "Finding a New Voice: Our Married Life After My Wife's Stroke," *Christian Century*, May 4, 2022, 15.

4. Ishmael, please recall, has his own rather bizarre history in Genesis; he was banished into the wilderness as a young boy with his mother, Hagar, due to interfamily jealousy, a rather dark chapter in the genealogy of Abraham found in Gen. 21:8–21. The reference to Ishmael here in the Joseph narrative is certainly a piece of the providential puzzle.

5. Anna Elkins, "If We Are All Unremarkable Angels," *Christian Century*, June 2024, 73.

6. See the powerful long-form essay by Larissa MacFarquhar, "The Fog," *New Yorker*, April 10, 2023, 32–49.

7. Frank G. Honeycutt, "Holy Detour," in *95 Prostheses: Appendages and Musings for the Body of Christ in Transition* (Eugene, OR: Cascade, 2018), 171–72.

Chapter 5

1. Again, note the roots of the word—*pro* (before) plus *videre* (to see). Literally, "a seeing ahead."

2. Dallas Willard, *The Divine Conspiracy: Rediscovering Our Hidden Life in God* (San Francisco: HarperSanFrancisco, 1998), 283.

Chapter 6

1. This startling reference seems to be overturned in Isa. 56:3–5. Perhaps Philip pointed out its proximity to the passage under consideration in the chariot that day.

2. This and other names in this story have been changed.

3. Annie Dillard, *For the Time Being* (New York: Knopf, 1999), 186–88.

Chapter 7

1. Portions of the opening section of this chapter, in slightly different form, first appeared in my article "The Bemusing Board-Game Beauty of the Bible," *Living Lutheran*, March-April 2023, 38–41.

2. Daniel Mason, *North Woods* (New York: Random House, 2023), 348–49.

3. Niall Williams, *This Is Happiness* (New York: Bloomsbury, 2019), 82.

4. "Finitude," writes Brent Strawn, "is a real problem for Qoheleth. In brief, he doesn't like it. It irks him that death is the great leveler of people." See Strawn, "Qoheleth Meets Covid-19," *Christian Century*, January 13, 2021, 26.

5. Jonathan Rosen, *The Best Minds: A Story of Friendship, Madness, and the Tragedy of Good Intentions* (New York: Penguin Press, 2023), 523.

6. *Concord (NC) Evening Tribune,* December 18, 1908, 1.

7. Ruth Gaines Honeycutt, *A Search for Yesterday* (self-published, 1998), 22.

8. Ron Rash, "Under Jocassee," in *Raising the Dead* (Oak Ridge, TN: Iris Press, 2002), 4.

RECOMMENDED READINGS

Dillard, Annie. *For the Time Being*. New York: Knopf, 1999.

El-Hai, Jack. *The Lobotomist: A Maverick Medical Genius and His Tragic Quest to Rid the World of Mental Illness*. Hoboken, NJ: Wiley & Sons, 2005.

Everett, Percival. *James*. New York: Doubleday, 2024. (fiction)

Harding, Paul. *This Other Eden*. New York: Norton, 2023. (fiction)

Honeycutt, Frank G. *Death by Baptism: Sacramental Liberation in a Culture of Fear*. Minneapolis: Fortress, 2021.

Jamison, Kay Redfield. *An Unquiet Mind: A Memoir of Moods and Madness*. New York: Knopf, 1995.

Lane, John. *Gullies of My People: An Excavation of Landscape and Family*. Athens, GA: University of Georgia Press, 2023.

Long, Thomas G. *What Shall We Say? Evil, Suffering, and the Crisis of Faith*. Grand Rapids: Eerdmans, 2011.

Mason, Daniel. *North Woods*. New York: Random House, 2023. (fiction)

Phillips, Jayne Anne. *Night Watch*. New York: Knopf, 2023. (fiction)

Rash, Ron. *Raising the Dead*. Oak Ridge, TN: Iris Press, 2002. (poetry)

Rosen, Jonathan. *The Best Minds: A Story of Friendship, Madness, and the Tragedy of Good Intentions*. New York: Penguin Press, 2023.

Williams, Niall. *This Is Happiness*. New York: Bloomsbury, 2019. (fiction)